More Power for Your Old PC

Upgrade Your System and Save $$

By Tina Rathbone

alpha books

A Division of Prentice Hall Computer Publishing
11711 North College, Carmel, Indiana 46032 USA

Alpha Books, 11711 N. College Ave., Carmel, IN 46032

International Standard Book Number:1-56761-023-4

Library of Congress Catalog Card Number: 92-74558

95 94 93 92   8 7 6 5 4 3 2 1

Interpretation of the printing code: the rightmost number of the first series of numbers is the year of the book's printing; the rightmost number of the second series of numbers is the number of the book's printing. For example, a printing code of 92-1 shows that the first printing of the book occurred in 1992.

Printed in the United States of America.

Publisher
Marie Butler-Knight

Managing Editor
Elizabeth Keaffaber

Product Development Manager
Lisa A. Bucki

Acquisitions Manager
Stephen R. Poland

Development Editor
Faithe Wempen

Production Editor
Lisa C. Hoffman

Copy Editor
Barry Childs-Helton

Editorial Assistant
Hilary J. Adams

Designer
Amy Peppler-Adams

Cover Illustrator
Steve Vanderbosch

Text Illustrator
Gary Varvel

Technical Line Art
Roger S. Morgan, Tim Groeling

Indexer
Jeanne Clark

Production Team
*Tim Cox, Mark Enochs,
Joelynn Gifford, Tim Groeling,
Phil Kitchel, Tom Loveman,
Michael J. Nolan, Carrie Roth,
Mary Beth Wakefield, Kelli Widdifield*

Special thanks to Hilary J. Adams for
ensuring the technical accuracy
of this book.

This book is dedicated to those who made the personal computer what it is today: easy (and fun) to upgrade. Also, it's dedicated to those PC owners who have the courage, curiosity, and commitment to get the most out of personal computing.

Tina Rathbone lives in San Diego, California with her husband, Andy and cat, Laptop. All three enjoy bird watching, fishing off the OB pier and tinkering with their CONFIG.SYS files.

Gary Varvel is a newspaper cartoonist who works with Macintosh computers (we'll forgive him). He resides in Danville, Indiana with his lovely wife, Carol, three children, a dog, and a bird. In the summer he plays the (alas!) dying game of fast-pitch softball.

Contents

Foreword   vii

Introduction   ix

Chapter 1   Inside Your PC: When to Upgrade
Your Computer   3

Chapter 2   Outside Your PC: When to Upgrade
Your Computing Environment   15

Chapter 3   Is Upgrading Worth Your While?   27

Chapter 4   Memory Upgrading   47

Chapter 5   A New Hard Drive   61

Chapter 6   Versatile Storage   71

Chapter 7   Updating the CPU and Motherboard   81

Chapter 8   More Ports, Please!   97

Chapter 9   Get the Picture   109

Chapter 10   Mastering the Art of Hard Copy   129

Chapter 11   Advancing Your Modeming Capabilities   147

Chapter 12   Fax with Your Computer   161

Chapter 13   The Multimedia Workstation   173

Chapter 14   Taking It on the Road   187

Chapter 15   Where to Buy Your Upgrades   203

Chapter 16   Got a Mechanic? Some Basic, Step-by-Step
              Installation Tips   219

Glossary   247

Index   255

Foreword

For people who love to shop, personal computers are great.

Especially for the first-time buyer, the initial purchase of a PC may be somewhat trying. After all, it's a lot of money, even if you did get that super deal.

Then the good times begin. Thereafter, the PC owner has an almost unlimited range of things that simply cry out to be bought. The PC magazines are filled with alluring gadgets and seductive supplements to your original system.

A lot of this stuff really doesn't cost all that much, and some items (like velour mouse-covers) are downright fun. There are also substantial investments—like higher-resolution printers, superior monitors, a zippier CPU, and external hard disk drives that might even be big enough to accommodate Windows or some of today's huge software.

All these things are upgrades. Even the dedicated shopper may find it difficult to choose, and for the hate-to-shopper, it can be torture.

And all this stuff costs money. An hour or two of light browsing in a computer discount store can add up to Visa Shock at the checkout counter.

Tina Rathbone is a thoroughly experienced upgrader and a hard-nosed, practical shopper. In *More Power for Your Old PC—Upgrade Your System and Save $$,* she provides an indispensable guide that can help the shopping-prone to avoid excess. The shopping-averse need it even more, because it enables them to define their requirements, plan their buy, overcome their inertia, and go for it.

Soak up the sensible advice in *More Power for Your Old PC* before you leap. Slip it into your handbag or jacket pocket (after buying it!) and refer to it quietly while you are in the computer store.

But use it. PC users buy all kinds of things because they fondly hope that their new acquisitions will improve productivity or make their system easier to use.

More Power for Your Old PC is much more sure-fire: It pays. The money you save will pay for the book again and again. Perhaps, just perhaps, it will save me so much that I can afford a laser printer instead of my ink-jet.

Norris Parker Smith

Editor-at-Large, *HPCwire*
(The High-Performance Computing electronic news "magazine")

September 1992

Introduction

Do the words *computer upgrade* induce the shivers? Nervous tics? The impulse to hop a red-eye to Hawaii? (Or, for Hawaiians, to catch the next flight to Akron, Ohio?)

Relax. You're not alone. Millions of PC owners experience fear and revulsion at the thought of upgrading. Why, occasionally even the most seasoned PC users greet the idea of prying open their system boxes with the same look of horror evoked by a glimpse of Frankenstein's lab . . . electrical ripples shooting out into the darkness, gobs of hoary cobwebs not altogether concealing the unspeakably sinister experiments . . . Igor (one of the more successful, uh, *projects*) hunched nearby.

Sure it's normal to fear upgrading. Yet most people eventually overcome their dread and upgrade anyway, once it dawns on them that the benefits from improving their computing setup outweigh the scarier "maybes."

Worrying Wastes Time

Enhancing your computing setup doesn't necessarily have to start with hours of deliberation over whether you can do it, or how. Right now, in your hands, you hold a huge advantage over most people. Keep this book by your side and you'll sidestep the hand-wringing phase altogether. Buoyed with confidence, bristling with energy, you'll be ready to fully enjoy the pleasures of a customized, powerful computing environment.

What, Me Worry?
Perhaps upgrading doesn't scare you in the least. That's great! Fearlessness, tempered with wisdom, will take you far with computers.

Hey, you're already fearless—this book provides the wisdom. Simply turn to the table of contents and seek out the chapters that interest you most. Or take a moment to check out the tips on "How to Use This Book," below, to get even more ideas on how this book can get you going.

Gee, I Dunno . . .
If the idea of boosting your PC's memory or adding an expansion card to your system makes you nervous, read a bit further in this introduction. Glance at the chapter descriptions to get a better idea of what upgrading means, and why it's worth the bother. Then turn to Chapter 1 and read the "Conquer Your Fears" section. You'll find a list of the

more common fears—along with the reasons why they're unfounded. When you're convinced upgrading's not so bad, come back to square one and get started in earnest.

A Word About You

Whether you're gung-ho or gun-shy about upgrading, this book assumes certain things about you.

- You own an IBM (or IBM-compatible) PC, or you're darned close to buying one. (If you haven't yet made your purchase, check out the section on upgradable PCs in Chapter 3—worth the price of this book alone.)

- You feel comfortable enough in your operating system (MS-DOS, most likely) to command your computer to do basic stuff such as making (and changing between) directories, getting a listing of files, starting and exiting programs, and restarting your PC.

- Your time is precious, so you expect this book to quickly summarize what's out there and what it can do for you. You seek pointers and pitfalls on the various types of upgrades, rather than detailed, product-specific installation guides.

- You're not a computer whiz, but you're intelligent. Most importantly, you're committed to improving your computing setup (or avoiding obsolescence when you purchase your PC), and you don't mind learning a little background if that leads to making the best choices.

How to Use This Book

You can march through this book chapter by chapter, or turn directly to the topic you want after a glance at the table of contents. If you need help diagnosing where your computer setup bogs down—and want some ideas for beefing it up—read around in Chapter 1, "Inside Your PC: When to Upgrade Your Computer," and Chapter 2, "Outside Your PC: When to Upgrade Your Computing Environment." Save yourself some grief by reading Chapter 3, "Is Upgrading Worth Your While?" early on.

Chapters 4 and 5 deal with the most common upgrades: memory and hard drives. Chapter 6 talks about floppy drives, tape back-up drives and other types of storage. Chapter 7 addresses adding a new motherboard, microprocessor, ROM-BIOS or math coprocessor. When it's time to add new ports, including the exotic but temperamental SCSI interface, check out Chapter 8. Those of you interested in beefing up your PC's display with a new video card or monitor should turn to Chapter 9.

If your systems cries out for a new printer or an advanced modem, you'll find what you're looking for in Chapters 10 and 11. Chapter 12 covers the convenience and increasing popularity of the fax card and the fax/modem combo. If multimedia always sounded too vague and complex to you, cut through all the jargon with a trip through Chapter 13, where you'll encounter fun stuff like sound cards and CD-ROM drives. For those of you interested in taking your show on the road, Chapter 14 looks at laptops, palmtops, and everything in-between.

If you seek shopping tips, turn to Chapter 15, "Searching for Upgrades." And don't overlook the nuts and bolts of upgrading, found in Chapter 16. (Don't forget to unplug your computer first!) The glossary and index will prove invaluable, whether you're shopping mail-order, trying to decipher a sales clerk's pitch, or wrestling with an installation manual.

Book Features

Look for special notes sprinkled throughout this book. These provide entertaining (and often essential) info, in an easy-to-spot, readable format. You can find them by visual cues such as shaded boxes and icons.

- *Bottom Line notes* suggest Best Buys and Don't Bothers.

- *Jargon notes* keep you shooting the crest of the waves of lingo you'll encounter while shopping.

- *History notes* sneak a peek at some of the more fascinating tidbits behind today's products.

- *Notes with distinctive icons* provide extra info on avoiding problems, or suggest a better way to accomplish a task.

How This Book Is Different

Bookstores bulge with computer upgrading books. But they all seem to approach the topic with a wrench in one hand and a diploma from MIT in the other. This one's different.

Knowing how to insert memory chips or a memory board is important, but it's even more important to know when to buy one or the other. Expansion cards and hard drives are indisputably considered as upgrades; most upgrading books can tell you how to install them. But this book counts specialty printers, high-speed modems, and high-resolution monitors as upgrades, too.

Loaded with pointers on how to tell whether your PC or some other component is bogging you down, this is the book for discovering when to upgrade the PC itself—or when it's time to upgrade your computing environment. Once you decide, you'll learn how to choose the best components and the best places to shop for them.

And, hey! You'll have fun, especially once the hard part—worrying over whether it's okay to upgrade—is over.

Acknowledgments

Many helping hands went into this book (don't worry, they came back out again . . .). Space doesn't allow me to mention all of you by name, so thank you!

A round of thanks goes to the good people at Alpha Books, and special thanks to Stephen Poland, Faithe Wempen, Lise (Lisa) Hoffman, and Barry Childs-Helton. I'd like to take this opportunity to applaud the vision of Alpha Books publisher Marie Butler-Knight, for creating this lively, unpretentious line of computer books.

This is the place to thank Andy Rathbone for his unflagging cheer and support, Ron Dippold (keeper of the net), and Norris Parker Smith, editor-at-large in perpetuity. To Linda Berez, plus Mark Wikholm, Steven Mizuno, Lutz Winkler, and Richard Ernst from ComputorEdge On-line: Thanks for sharing your motherboard trials and tribulations! I'd also like to express gratitude to Maria, Alice and Rhett.

Warm, alphabetical-order thanks go out to the many PC industry professionals who took time out to discuss (and occasionally ship) their products for this book: Gale Blackburn, Boca Research, Inc.; Laura Gaittens, Intel Corp.; Rebecca Herst, Acer America Corp.; Mike Jurs, (NEC) Golin/Harris Communications, Inc.; Elizabeth Kemper, Intel

Corp.; Lee Kufchak, PC-Kwik Corp.; Robert Kutnick, Amkly Systems, Inc. (who drove down all the way from Irvine); Denise McLaughlin, Dell Computer Corp.; Claire Merriam, Media Vision, Inc.; Forrest (Woody) Monroy, Conner Peripherals; Bruce Roemmich, Colorado Memory Systems, Inc.; Diane Scott, Rasterops Corp.; Ron Seide, Kingston Technology Corp.; Jill Shanks, Dell Computer Corp.; Randy Stolz, Intel Corp.; Joe Stunkard, Artisoft, Inc.; Steve Williams, Alpha Research Corp.

Last but not least, thanks to Dan Gookin, one of the first computer journalists to discover that computers don't have to be "dull and boring."

Trademarks

All terms mentioned in this book that are known to be trademarks or service marks are listed below. In addition, terms suspected of being trademarks or service marks have been appropriately capitalized. Alpha Books cannot attest to the accuracy of this information. Use of a term in this book should not be regarded as affecting the validity of any trademark or service mark.

286, 386, 486, and Intel SL are trademarks of Intel Corp.

386 Pro is a trademark of Links.

386MAX is a trademark of Qualitas.

Above Board, Intel SL, Snap-In, SnapIn 386, and RapidCAD are trademarks of Intel Corp.

America Online is a service mark of America Online, Inc.

Amkly and Power-Drive Pak are registered trademarks of Amkly Systems, Inc.

ChipUp is a trademark of Acer America Corp.

Compaq is a registered trademark of Compaq Computer Corp.

CompuServe Information Service is a registered trademark of CompuServe, Inc. and H&R Block, Inc.

Dell 450DE is a trademark and Dell 450DE PC is a registered trademark of Dell Computer Corp.

DeskJet, HP95, HP LaserJet, LaserJet II, LaserJet III, are trademarks of Hewlett-Packard.

DESQview, Manifest, and Quarterdeck QEMM/386 are trademarks of Quarterdeck Office Systems.

Disk Test is a trademark and Norton Utilities is a registered trademark of Peter Norton Computing (a subsidiary of Symantec Corp.).

Ecosys is a trademark of Kyocera.

GeoWorks is a trademark of GeoWorks.

MaxFax II is a trademark of Macronix.

MS-DOS, TrueType, Windows 3.1, Word for Windows, and Microsoft Windows are registered trademarks of Microsoft Corp.

Norton's DiskTest and Speed Disk are registered trademarks of Symantec Corp.

OS/2 is a registered trademark and IBM, IBM PC, AT, and XT are trademarks of International Business Machines Corp.

PC-Kwik, Power Disk, Power Pak, and SuperPC-Kwik are trademarks of PC-Kwik Corp.

Portfolio is a trademark of Atari Corp.

PostScript is a registered trademark of Adobe Systems, Inc.

Power-Drive Pack is a trademark of Amkly Systems.

PrintCache is a trademark of LaserTool.

SpinWrite is a trademark of Gibson Research.

Stacker is a trademark of Stac Electronics.

SX/Now! is a trademark of Kingston Technology Corp.

TrueType is a trademark of Apple Computer, Inc.

UNIX is a registered trademark of AT&T Bell Laboratories.

W5086 is a trademark of Weitek.

WinFax is a trademark of Delrina.

Wizard is a trademark of Sharp Electronics Corp.

Inside Your PC: When to Upgrade Your Computer

When most people think of upgrading their PCs, they think of opening the system box and replacing a faulty, worn or obsolete component with a shiny new one . . . perhaps uttering strange and colorful murmurings as they work. (They didn't have this book!)

Upgrading the PC itself is only half the upgrading equation (as you'll see after you read Chapter 2). But it's an important part.

Knowing how to update older components in the system box is important if you want to keep getting the most out of your PC. In this chapter, we'll see how some typical systems have bogged down over time—and how their owners diagnosed and performed the appropriate upgrade. When a particular section seems to describe your case, simply turn to the chapter dedicated to that upgrade.

But first, I've a promise to keep. Anyone who still doubts that they can do it themselves will feel better after reading the next section. (The Joe Confidents in the group can skip it.)

Conquer Your Doubts

This may be painful to hear, but some PC users light up at the thought of tearing out old components and snapping, sliding, or screwing in new ones. For the rest of us, fear of upgrading stems from a variety of reasons—or *un*reasons, to be precise (since there are few *real* reasons not to upgrade a PC). Let's tackle the most common objections one by one, and in doing so, banish forever the cobwebs of anguish and doubt.

You're Gonna Laugh at Me, but What's Upgrading?

To the newer user, and even some old hands, the U-word sounds vague and ominous. What exactly *is* upgrading, and how can you tell if or when your PC needs it? For the purposes of this book, upgrading your computer means two things:

- First, a typical upgrade might be a simple replacement of a slow, worn, or broken part inside your PC with a newer, more powerful one. For example, you might remove the older, slower, low-capacity memory chips from your motherboard's RAM slots, and insert faster, higher-capacity chips in their place. And maybe add a few more to fill out your RAM capacity. (Read on in this chapter to find more examples of upgrading the PC itself.)

- The second way to upgrade is to add a completely new component to your setup. A good example is buying and setting up a desktop scanner, so you can scan and use graphics from outside sources. (Chapter 2 talks more about when it's time to teach your PC some new tricks with outside stuff.)

How Do I Know It's Time to Upgrade?

In the end, both types of upgrades beef up a PC so it can perform tasks better. That answers the other Big Question: How can I tell when it's time to upgrade? When your computer system is not meeting your goals or running the software you want to run, or is otherwise balking at the types of tasks you want it to perform, it's time to upgrade it.

I'll Fry My Hair Even Worse Than a Home Perm . . .

Sure, they're precision-engineered electronic devices. But PCs aren't as delicate as they seem. The careful advice in each chapter of this book will build your confidence level. Besides, people don't get electrical shocks when they're careful to unplug everything—at both ends—before touching anything but the cord.

I Don't Know My PC Well Enough . . .

Most people don't buy a car planning to become automotive mechanics. And most folks don't buy a PC with the aim of becoming computer engineers. You don't need to work at Joe's Garage to know when your car needs new tires or a better stereo, right? Well, you don't need a degree in computer science to upgrade your PC. Just think about your needs, see where your PC's not meeting those needs, and compare the user scenarios throughout this book with your own situation.

Jär-gen:

You don't have to read a New Age self-help book to ground yourself. Humans shuffle around in a constant flow of static electricity. Grounding means discharging that static electricity by tapping on bare metal, wearing a grounding wrist strap, or just hanging onto your PC's chassis. Since static electricity is harmful to your chips and components, ground yourself frequently when upgrading.

NOTE

PCs are modular, a fancy word that means they're designed so that many parts can be removed and new ones inserted. In fact, some hardy souls have been known to build their own PCs out of parts they buy at computer stores or through the mail. (Do not try this at home.) As long as you're calm and patient—and grounded, if you're opening the system box—and you follow the advice in this book, you'll be safe (and so will your PC).

My Buddy Says This Hunk of Junk's Not Worth Upgrading!

This may be true (gasp). Some of the earliest PCs will never be sleek 486s, no matter how many new goodies you stick inside. If you have any doubts, turn to Chapter 3, "Is Upgrading Worth Your While?" If your PC is listed among the Don't Bothers, keep reading in Chapter 3 for advice on buying a PC that's upgradable.

Time to Upgrade!

It seems like only yesterday the UPS guy practically banged down your door, groaning under the weight of the parcels in his arms. You felt a tinge of excitement in your esophagus even as you signed on line #4 for your new PC. After lugging the mondo boxes upstairs and setting everything up, you wondered why you'd waited this long to take the personal computer plunge.

At first, your new PC seemed almost custom-designed. You found software that solved each new task, and your hardware ran the software well. But

You hardly ever hear of someone replacing a worn part with the same exact part. That goes against the nature of personal computing— which, at its heart, is geared towards a dizzying, incessant flow of newer, brighter, faster, more powerful products. Now, you don't have to buy into the techno-lust mentality, just as you don't have to drive around town with a license plate holder that reads: "I'd Rather Be Shopping at Nordstrom." But, hey, as long as you have the system box open, replace the clunker with the latest part. Your ol' PC deserves it. And you'll enjoy its new zest!

BOTTOM LINE

slowly, almost imperceptibly, your PC started failing you. Bogging down—especially once you upgraded to that hot new Windows operating environment. You caught yourself looking at other systems—the first stolen glimpses leading to open, longing gazes. You may have found yourself in one or more of the following scenarios.

Out of Memory!

One day Debbie chanced upon Chris spell checking a document. "How'd you do that from within your word processor?" she demanded. "I always get a weird 'Out of Memory' message, so I have to quit my word processor before loading the spell checker."

Chris smiled. "It's really easy," he said. "You just need more memory."

Just about everybody's heard "more memory," either from computing friends or from their computing screen. In fact, adding more memory ranks near the top of commonly performed computer upgrades.

Many popular programs (like Microsoft Windows) require a computer with *at least* 2 megabytes (MB) of Random Access Memory (RAM). When your PC runs software, RAM gives the microprocessor a place to store instructions and data it's not using at the moment. Because today's software is large and unwieldy, today's computers need correspondingly more RAM space. Extra RAM can boost your computer's performance in other ways too, such as speeding up hard disk access (since the hard disk dumps stored data onto RAM first, where it's gobbled up by the microprocessor).

Basically, adding memory means just that: buying little black "chips" of memory and plugging them into special sockets inside your computer, just like dropping a slice of bread into the toaster. Well, almost. Just as that thick slice of French bread won't fit in your cool Salvation Army toaster, not all memory chips work in all computers. And, for some systems, the best way to go is to add an expansion card with slots for memory chips. Then there's always memory caching and other stuff—confusing for you, but great for your PC.

Not Enough Room to Install That Neat New Program

"The magazine review said this is the best word processor ever written. The reviewer said he even found 'inchoate' in the thesaurus," Jeff called out to his wife as he inserted Disk 7 and obeyed the installation program's prompt. Bing! Jeff looked at the error message on his monitor:

If your PC balks when you try to run new programs, check the software's box (or manual) to see how much RAM it needs to run right. Then boot up your PC and count its memory (instructions in Chapter 4). If your system falls short, keep reading in Chapter 4 for tips on memory.

BOTTOM LINE

9

```
Disk Full - Unable to complete operations.
```

Ten years ago, ten copies of a word processor fit onto one floppy disk. Today's crop of powerhouses come with a powerful crop of disks that proffer thesauruses, grammar checkers, and even graphics modules. Word for Windows, for example, can consume 15 MB of hard disk space. Why, the Windows operating environment takes up 15MB for itself! Suddenly that 40MB hard drive looks peanut-sized.

Today's hard drives find more than one way to dispel that bogged-down feeling: Besides holding tons more data, they access it faster—diminishing the traditional lag of these highly mechanical (read: slow) components. New hard drives sport more intelligent controllers, too, so they work better with today's software. *Caching disk controller* products offer yet another way to speed data access.

If "Disk Full" is giving you an earful, or the hard disk's red light glows longer than the busy intersection's at rush hour, seek out hard drive and disk caching upgrades in Chapter 5.

BOTTOM LINE

Other Common System Upgrades

Some other upgrade signals come in loud and clear. If your ability to take work home is thwarted by the fact that the office PC's packing a 3 1/2-inch floppy drive while yours is a 5 1/4-inch relic, time to upgrade! (Turn to Chapter 6.)

If your new CAD program demands a math coprocessor and you haven't quite gotten around to installing one, time to upgrade! (Turn to Chapter 7.)

Links 386 Pro, Windows 3.1 in Enhanced Mode, and the OS/2 operating system require a 386 or better microprocessor. To use these programs, so do you. Time to upgrade! (Turn to Chapter 7.)

In This Chapter, You Learned . . .

Fearing computer upgrades is common. It's even okay—as long as you get over it quickly so you can upgrade and enjoy your PC! Upgrading is okay, too. Moreover, it was *meant to be.*

Upgrading means two things: replacing old PC components with new ones, and adding completely new peripherals and equipment to your PC setup. Typical user scenarios showed you some "time to upgrade" signals for the first type of upgrading: replacing worn, broken, or obsolete parts inside the PC with new ones. Look to the next chapter for signs of when to add cool stuff to your setup.

Chapter 1 Checklist: Assessing Your PC

• What tasks would you like your PC to be able to accomplish?

_____

_____

_____

• What software does these tasks?

_____

_____

_____

• What level of PC hardware does this software need in order to run well?

_____

_____

_____

• Does any software product produce this enhancement? (Printer manager, hard disk optimizer, etc.?)

_____

_____

_____

• Where does your PC fall short? List below:

Task:	Software requires:	My PC has:	Candidates for Upgrade:
_____	_____	_____	_____
_____	_____	_____	_____
_____	_____	_____	_____
_____	_____	_____	_____

Notes: _____

_____

_____

_____

_____

_____

_____

_____

Outside Your PC: When to Upgrade Your Computing Environment

Your PC itself is doing fine. You've a speedy microprocessor, a decent bank of memory chips, and your hard disk seems to be gulping down everything you throw on it. Yet somehow your computer isn't up to the job.

Chances are, it's not your PC that's lagging. It may be your computing environment instead. This chapter covers upgrades that boost your PC into whole new realms of productivity. Read through these examples to glean some ideas on how to max out your own system. Best of all, some of these upgrades don't even require you to open the case.

Hottest New Game Comes on a CD-ROM

The minute Barry opened the cool golf game's shrinkwrap, he despised his old computer's low-density floppy drives. The game came on high-density disks! Barry wouldn't soon forget the three-week wait for replacement disks. But the worst part was seeing all the guys at work standing around the water cooler, bragging about their pars and birdies.

When Barry bought his new PC, he'd made darn sure to get both 3 1/2-inch and 5 1/4-inch high-density floppy drives, figuring he'd be set for life. Until he ordered his latest game, that is—the one with spoken dialogue as well as musical scores. It came in the mail—on one of those funky new CD-ROM discs!

CD-ROM discs hold more data than floppies; they're just made that way. That's why it doesn't take a genius to figure out that if software keeps getting any bigger, CD-ROMs, not floppies, will await you inside those shrinkwrapped boxes. Already, some programs come in special CD-ROM versions that hold more pictures or sounds (true space hogs) than the standard version.

Installing a CD-ROM drive happens one of two ways, depending on whether you buy an external unit or one that fits into one of your PC's disk drive bays. For tips on when to buy one (they're not just for gamers), which one to buy, and how to buy it—as well as how to install it—turn to Chapter 13.

Software That Talks (with a Sound Card)

"My computer has a speaker," Jennifer told the technical support person over the phone. "So I figured the software would just use that speaker to talk through. What's a 'sound card?'"

Jennifer forgot to examine the software's box before buying, to make sure her hardware could run the software. She thought the sound part was a neat perk; when she heard it required a separate component, she decided it wasn't worth shelling out the $150 bucks just to hear words.

Hector, a non-native speaker of English, bought the same dictionary software. He sprang for a sound card, though, since hearing standard American pronunciation would help him master his new language. He settled on a card with a built-in amplifier. Then he hooked up some garage-sale speakers to his new setup. The voice sounded great! Later that evening, some friends brought over the latest adventure game. After hearing the trolls roar and the witch cackle in full stereo, Hector couldn't believe he'd waited so long for a sound card.

Sound cards give an audio dimension to your PC—for not very much money. Serious gamers wouldn't be without sound, but you can find plenty of productivity software jumping on the sound band-wagon. Currently, Windows users can plant recorded speech into their spreadsheets to explain the basis for cell 31, for example, or to add comments to their word processing documents.

Scientists confirm that visual cues assist learning. Perhaps this helps explain the surge of graphics enlivening our computers. Sound reinforces the message, too. The growing popularity of business presentations that employ sound, color, and animation proves it. (We're the Hanna-Barbera/Disney/Warner Bros. Generation!) Teach your PC to talk after checking out Chapter 13.

Slow in Windows

"Windows is great," Jack thought to himself as he drummed his fingers along the desk. "With so many programs on the screen at the same time, I can cut the map right out of the paint program and stick it on the party flier." He drummed his fingers a little faster. "If only those programs would get on the screen."

The wacky world of the Microsoft Windows operating environment can inspire a burst of creativity, but only after a burst of curses about how slow the PC seems. Graphics can deflate the sails of the best PCs, and Windows puts a strain on the fastest computer. Luckily, upgrades like math coprocessors—or even graphics accelerator cards that contain processors—can help. These "Windows-tailored" expansion cards can make the wind blow, carrying that creative cargo across the room and into your document.

If you use lots of text-only programs and run software out of MS-DOS, a Windows accelerator isn't the upgrade you need. But if you do Windows, computer-assisted design, desktop publishing, or computer art, take a second look at the way your PC draws images to the screen. If it resembles a lava lamp on tranquilizers, you might need a math coprocessor or a graphics accelerator card. Turn to Chapter 7 to see if you'd benefit from a math chip, or Chapter 9 to learn more about graphics video accelerators.

Backing Up's a Pain!

Harriet enjoyed commanding MS-DOS to show her how much space was left on her hard disk. She felt more than a little proud to know that her PC was the first in the company to be fitted with one of those new, high-capacity hard drives. She must have needed it, too, for all 340 megabytes filled up soon enough.

The one drawback was backing up her work. Even with special back-up software, that huge drive took forever! Her wrist was wearing out from all the floppy swapping. Harriet knew she was courting disaster, but she decided to turn her back on backing up for a couple of months.

No, Harriet's hard drive didn't crash. Fortunately, she saw an ad for a tape-backup unit before that happened. Her PC had plenty of drive bays left, so she ordered an internal unit and set to work installing it herself. The manual actually seemed to be written in English! Thanks to the Windows Launcher, she could install the unit's software from within Windows—and everything worked by clicking on icons. Harriet loved the Scheduler option that let her arrange for an automatic, "no-brainer" backup each midnight.

Tape backup drives present an affordable, automated solution to an age-old problem: how to restore a PC's programs and data after a drive crashes or a system halts. Business users in particular should consider this upgrade. If backing up's got your back up against a wall, turn to Chapter 6.

Fax Cards Deal a Winning Hand

The roundabout way: Type a letter on your PC. Print it out. Trudge over to the fax machine. Wait in line for Max to stop gabbing and start faxing his darn letter. Fax your letter to Joe's fax machine. Wait for his machine's busy signal to stop. Re-fax your letter to Joe's fax machine. The direct route: Type a letter on your PC, type in Joe's fax number, and press a button. Voilà! It's instantly faxed to Joe, or re-faxed until it gets through—at speeds higher than many modems—even as you perform other computing tasks.

Fax cards are here to stay. And, thanks to them, perhaps the "paperless office" that computers were supposed to enable is finally here, too.

Imagine your fax card on the receiving end. Mabel sends you her fax, you read it, and then ping! It's gone with the press of a Del key. No curly fax paper to make you want to kill the sender. No piles of useless junk faxes touting *Round-trip Fares to Mexico, Only $499!* No retyping! Infrequent faxers won't have to dedicate a phone line, either. And many fax cards double as modems. To find out more, turn to Chapter 12.

Other Upgrade Options

No one would argue that buying a laptop counts as enhancing your computing setup. Yet who has time to keep up with all the confusing jargon? Turn to Chapter 14 for the low-down on mobile computing. Maybe you road-warrior types need a portable printer or want to fax on the fly. Portable components can be found in the chapter dedicated to that subject: for example, portable modems under "Modems," or portable printers under "Printers."

Suddenly your application requires graphics printout. How do you squeeze that from a lesser printer? Time to upgrade that hard-copy hog. Turn to Chapter 10 to see what printer will best perform your tasks.

Maybe you need a monitor that's a match for the new video card you bought, or some advice on upgrading your software. Turn to the table of contents and get started today improving your system setup.

In This Chapter, You Learned . . .

Software is advancing—seemingly by the minute. To keep up with it— and actually be able to do what it promises—you can't avoid buying new equipment for your PC. Adding peripherals like fax modems and sound cards are a big part of upgrading your system, as is buying a state-of-the-art monitor or printer. Scan the chapter headings to find your ultimate upgrade. To learn when you might not really need to upgrade, read on.

Chapter 2 Checklist: Assessing Your PC's Accessories:

• What tasks would you like your PC to be able to accomplish?

_____

_____

_____

• What software does these tasks?

_____

_____

_____

• What PC add-ons (scanner, modem, etc.) does this software need in order to run well?

_____

_____

_____

• Where does your PC fall short? List below:

Task:	Software Product:	Requires this hardware component:
_____	_____	_____
_____	_____	_____
_____	_____	_____
_____	_____	_____

Notes: _____

_____

_____

_____

_____

_____

_____

SNIFF

Is Upgrading Worth Your While?

Upgrading your PC's almost always a Good Thing. Yet, even in the supremely logical world of computers, there are few absolutes. Depending on your current system and your software's needs, you may be better off chucking your old setup altogether and going with newer technology.

Before you dump it in the ash can, try boosting your PC's performance with a few of the software and hardware tricks you'll find here. If you do opt for a new system, or if you don't yet own a PC, be sure to read about upgradable PCs and the recommendations for Windows "workstations" in the last part of this chapter.

When Not to Upgrade

Sometimes upgrading just isn't worthwhile. Buying a new PC is the best solution when:

- Replacing the old, slowpoke components would cost more than buying an entirely new system. Note that prices for entry-level systems are lower than you'd think. Look for 386DX systems, including faster hard disk, plenty of expansion slots, a new monitor/video card combo, and even a mouse, for under $900. For comparison's sake, simply adding a new hard drive runs about $300, and you still haven't added in all the other parts.

Jär-gen:

286 and 386 are nicknames for the 80286 and 80386 microprocessor chips in PCs. A 386SX is a less-expensive, slightly less-powerful variant of the 80386. You need at least a 386SX to get the most from Microsoft Windows and many other multitasking programs. While we're at it, a 386DX is just another name for a full-strength 386.

- You own a no-name or lesser-known brand of 286 computer, but need the multitasking capabilities of a 386SX or better. You'll have a hard time upgrading your microprocessor, since most of the companies who make chip upgrades target their products for a specific line of high-end PCs (for example, Kingston Technology's SX/Now!). A 286-to-386SX system upgrade *may* work with a lesser-known brand of computer, but the product is guaranteed to be compatible only with certain high-end brands (Compaq and IBM, specifically). The same thing applies to Intel's Snap-In upgrade products, which target True-Blue IBMs.

- You want to beef up your XT with an advanced hard disk, a large, fast video card, or another 16-bit (or better) expansion card. The most advanced hard drive controllers were designed to make use of the 80286 chip and its 16-bit bus. (Most of the other newer devices also shun the XT's older slower 8-bit bus.) To use some of the newer add-ons, you'll have to upgrade your motherboard, too.

Jär-gen:

An XT refers to a computer with an 8086 microprocessor. These dinosaurs are all but extinct, because their capabilities are so far behind the advanced microprocessors on the market today.

You can see that upgrading isn't the cure-all for every PC malady. Even upgrading a 286 chip to a 386SX leaves you stuck with slower RAM chips, a poky hard drive, and possibly an outdated video standard. In contrast, an actual, shiny 386 system contains all these updated components, and offers you more for your money.

You're Trying to Talk Me Out of This?

Upgrading is still a viable solution for many PC bottlenecks. Especially when you have a firm grasp of the improvement you want to see in your PC, you know what's possible and what's not, and you're willing to take things step-by-step. After all, purchasing a component here and there is much easier than plunking down the plastic for the killer, sticker-shocking new system. And that 286 would positively scream with a new 386 motherboard inside.

Besides, many of the newest PCs target hardware-hungry Microsoft Windows and other graphical software. Well, many folks are not the least bit interested in running Windows or its spinoffs. They speed along in fast, command-line-ready DOS software. But maybe they want to speed along a bit faster, by taking the upgrade route.

Low-Cost Upgrade Tricks

There's a zillion ways to put off major hardware purchases. These software (and minor hardware) tricks won't put off the upgrade for-ever—sooner or later, you'll find yourself outgrowing them and on your way to the computer store.

Upgrading Your System Software

Maybe you're running an ancient version of the MS-DOS operating system. Or perhaps you've longed to try Microsoft Windows 3.1, the hotshot graphical user interface (GUI) on everyone's lips. Each has ways to enhance the way your PC handles everyday chores. Teamed together, these two programs can make your computing sessions easier and more fun.

DOS version 5.0 or greater can give you more memory—even if you don't buy the actual chips. See, your first 640K of memory is the most important because that's the coveted section all the DOS programs try to play in. DOS version 5.0 took the bold step of loading all its DOS system files into a different part of your memory. That leaves more of the 640K memory for your programs. If you're not using DOS 5.0, it's time to check it out.

If you want to benefit from extra RAM by running several programs at once, you might check out Windows. Windows can download a file from an on-line service in the background, for instance, while you're writing a letter in the foreground. Don't get carried away, though. Windows needs lots of memory (2 MB or more) to function effectively.

Don't have a lot of memory and still want a graphical user interface? Then check out GeoWorks. It runs on an XT (Windows needs a 286 or higher) and doesn't need as much memory as Windows. It brings a GUI to a bare-bones machine.

Extra Memory and What You Can Do with It

After new system software, your second upgrade act should be to add more memory to your PC's motherboard, or to a RAM expansion card. (Turn to Chapter 4 to see how it's done.) You'll need to install a software *memory manager*, and then the extra on-board RAM can be used in a variety of ways to enhance your system (this approach can even work with an old XT or other 8088 system).

- *RAM disks:* The fastest hard drive may not be a disk at all. Check out the section called "Faster Storage with Good Old DOS" later in this chapter to see how to put your spare RAM to work as a disk drive.

- *Print spoolers:* You can free up the CPU to do other work while it's waiting for the slow printer by installing software known as a *print spooler.* It works by setting aside a portion of your PC's spare RAM. There the print job waits, feeding itself to the printer a chunk at a time.

NOTE

One spooler, LaserTool's PrintCache, can set itself up to run under DOS or Windows, and offers the added feature of compressing graphics files to nudge your old printer along.

- *Disk caches:* Writing your work to disk can take up a lot of the CPU's time and energy. A disk cache writes to disk in the background, freeing up the CPU for other work. The cache uses spare memory as a storage space and monitors the disk carefully, watching to see what info it needs. If any needed data is already in the storage space, it can be read from there instead, speeding up disk accesses immensely. In many cases, a good software cache can perform as well as expensive hardware disk cache controllers.

NOTE

One highly-rated product, PC-Kwik's SuperPC-Kwik, achieves speed without delaying disk writes, a "fudge" that some cache products use to gain speed. A delay in writing to disk could prove dastardly to your data in the event of a power outage (or accidental flick of the Off switch), since the data is in RAM until saved to disk.

Integrated Memory Helpers

Some software programs, such as PC-Kwik's Power Pak, provide several memory helpers: a disk cache, a RAM disk, a print spooler, and a keyboard/screen accelerator, among others. The benefit to an integrated utility like this is that the various modules share memory with each other—and with DOS programs and Windows when they need it. You still have to buy a memory manager program. Plus, some users will miss out on the sense of achievement they'd get by setting up fixes like RAM disks themselves. Then again, for $75, you could use the time you saved playing with RAM disks to pay some attention to your lonely family members . . .

Hard Disk "Doubling"

Compression software can squeeze data down to about half its size, essentially doubling the size of your hard disk. These products present an excellent value: They average $100, compared with $300 or so for a new 100MB hard drive. One compression product, Stac Electronics' Stacker, stores files on a single Stacker file, which foolhardy DOS sees as a hard disk. Stacker works with Windows, and soon it will work with OS/2. The "stacked" disk has a slower access rate than a regular hard disk; an optional Stacker hardware board ($200) can bring the access time back to nearly normal.

Be sure to back up your entire hard drive before installing any up-grade, especially a compression product.

The Optimized Disk

Nothing bogs down a computing session faster than seeking information on disk, especially if the disk is *fragmented* (patches of data have been lost over time).

DOS stores data anywhere it finds a place, and as you repeatedly write to or erase the disk, it becomes peppered with data vacancies (or "fragmented," in disk parlance). Before you sprint down to the computer store, let some of these software solutions sprint over your hard disk.

- DOS's CHKDSK will look for file allocation and directory listing errors.

- Norton's DiskTest will do a test read of every sector.

- PC-Kwik's Power Disk rates as the speediest disk de-fragmenter. PC Tools (Compress) and Norton Utilities (Speed Disk) are other reliable defragmenting programs.

- Gibson Research's SpinWrite will do an in-depth analysis/test of the disk's surface; it can also hasten data transfer by modifying your hard disk controller's *interleave* (which affects the number of times the disk must revolve before an entire disk track can be scanned).

NOTE

OS/2 users can't benefit from standard defragmenting utilities. OS/2 uses a different method from DOS to store data on a disk. This method, called High Performance File System (HPFS), actually minimizes disk fragmentation as it works, so you don't need to optimize as often. GammaTech makes a utility package for OS/2 that includes disk management modules.

Back Up with Good Old DOS

It's slow, but it's sure, and it's already part of MS-DOS: the BACKUP utility. Before you experience a hard drive failure or begin an upgrade, sit down with a stack of floppies—DOS manual turned to the BACKUP utility's page. You don't even need to format the floppies first. If your hard drive should fail, you can use DOS's RESTORE utility to restore the files you've backed up. DOS will even prompt you to insert the floppies in the right order. Not as fast or sexy as a dedicated tape-backup unit, or even commercial backup software—but, hey, the price is right.

Faster Storage Using Good Old DOS

Faster than a speeding hard disk! It's a RAM drive, a way to use part of your PC's memory as a pretend, or *virtual*, hard disk. A RAM disk is faster than a real hard disk because the information held in the RAM disk is already in memory—bypassing the (comparatively) time-consuming process engaged in by the traditional hard disk as it finds, fetches, and stores data into RAM for the microprocessor's use.

How do people use a RAM drive? Many PC gurus copy a program in which they're working over to a RAM drive they create. Other experts recommend storing certain types of programs that involve unusually heavy disk access into a RAM drive; for example, a word processor's spell checker, Window's temporary files, or a programming language's program library. Using a RAM drive in these ways can speed up the way the software works considerably.

There's nothing new or strange about using spare RAM in this way. In fact, good old DOS already contains a special program, RAMDRIVE.SYS, that lets you create the RAM drive. To create a "practice" RAM drive for yourself, consult your DOS manual's index, under RAMDRIVE.SYS, or turn to Chapter 16.

No discussion of RAM drives would be complete without these cautionary notes:

- Any files you're working in *must be saved often to your actual hard disk.* That's because the information on the RAM disk exists only in the volatile RAM memory that disappears when your PC's power is shut off.

- When you create the RAM drive, it appears on your PC as a new drive letter. If your normal hard disk letter is C:, the RAM drive will appear as D:. Since RAM drive D: disappears the minute the PC powers down, gurus working with a program installed on the RAM drive know to save their work to real-disk C:, instead.

- Also, you must copy your working program over to the RAM drive yourself. Your software can't automatically sense the new, "pretend" drive's presence.

Sound *Sans* Sound Card

Sound files with a .WAV extension come bundled in Microsoft Windows version 3.1. If you want to hear the sounds, but don't have a sound card, a Windows 3.1 sound driver called SPEAK.EXE can help. Locate the file through user groups, shareware distributors, or via CompuServe, among other electronic bulletin board systems (BBSs).

Software Fonts

Windows users will enjoy upgrading their printer's capabilities by adding TrueType fonts. Several vendors sell them, including Microsoft itself. TrueType fonts are scalable, meaning you can size them to your specifications. They work with any printer that works with Windows.

Adding a Switch Box

This last isn't exactly a software fix, but presents an inexpensive and easy way to load your PC with even more neat serial devices. For well under $25, you can add something called a *switch box* to a single serial port (COM1:). The box sports several "slots" where you can plug in as many devices as you want. Be sure to connect only those devices you wouldn't run simultaneously, since only one at a time can occupy the COM1: interrupt space. (See Chapter 8 for grisly details on interrupts.) If you take this route, keep plenty of wire twisty-ties handy to organize all the cables.

Anticipating Future Upgrades

If you opt for buying a new system, don't get stuck this time around! Scan the following sections to learn about upgradable PCs. Here, too, you can find out about the type of system Windows needs (demands). If you don't yet own a PC, take a look at some of the upgradables on the shelves.

You can download fonts from CompuServe and other BBSs, often for free, or for a low shareware fee payable to the author.

BOTTOM LINE

Upgradable PCs

Several PC makers have come out with systems designed in advance to hedge against computer obsolescence. Here are a few examples.

Acer's ChipUp system lets you upgrade the microprocessor by snapping a new chip into a vacant socket on the motherboard. The old microprocessor stays in place, and the two chips work together (so you can't recoup part of your original investment by selling the old microprocessor).

Amkly Systems makes an extremely modular system. The new chip is on a proprietary card that fits into a chip card slot on the expansion board. Nearby, a second, microprocessor-dedicated fan cools it. Unique to Amkly is the Power-Drive Pack that holds four drives and a 200-watt power supply, and lifts out at the snap of a lever (as shown in Figure 3.1). Inside, the design allows for drive connectors and cables to nest in a thoughtfully designed recess, safe from hasty lid removals. The PC's BIOS can be upgraded through software, an unusual feature known as *flash ROM* (a recessed button must first be pushed, to prevent unauthorized access to your ROM). Flash ROM makes it easy to tell your PC there's been an upgrade.

If you don't yet own a PC, check out The Most PC for Your Money (Alpha Books, 1992). This easy-to-read book will help you select your first PC with confidence.

BOTTOM LINE

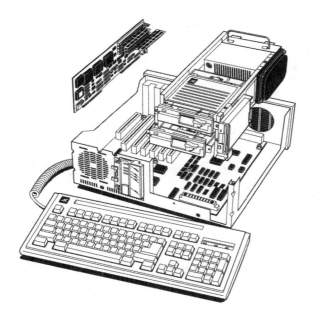

Figure 3.1

PCs like this Amkly are designed for easy access. (Illustration courtesy of Amkly Systems, Inc.)

Dell Computer makes an upgradable line similar to Amkly's. Want to upgrade to a faster chip? Then pull out the little card with the old chip, and slip in the new card with the new chip! Easy action, and you can still sell the old chip. The smart system instantly knows there's been a new processor added, right at bootup. Plus, the motherboard contains two serial ports, a parallel port, and a Super VGA port, leaving all six slots free for anything you want to plug in there. Fun. The other advantage to Dell's system is that it comes from a reputable, widely-established company that will probably still be around when it's time to buy your upgraded processor card.

If you're in the market for a new (or a first) PC, be sure to compare some upgradables. And keep these buying tips in mind.

- If the chip is on a proprietary expansion card, will the manufacturer be around in a few years to sell you a new one?

- Several years from now, will you pay more for an upgraded processor than for a comparable, new system?

- Can you sell the old microprocessor (or microprocessor expansion card)?

- How difficult is it to install the upgrade card/chip? Do you have to tear everything else out of your system before you can upgrade?

Buying a "Windows Workstation"

Lately the PC outlets seem filled with systems that claim to be *Windows workstations*. When you decide to succumb to the Windows Syndrome (More, More, More), check to make sure the PC's claims are founded in fact, or you could end up with just a plain, average (but well-marketed) PC. If the Windows workstation is upgradable, you could be tied to a single supplier for future upgrades.

At the time of this writing, PC pundits recommend Windows systems as nothing less than a 386/20 with at least a 100MB hard disk and 4MB of RAM, a Windows accelerator video card, and an SVGA monitor (preferably larger than the standard 14-inch model). That's the minimum model. The preferred system: 386/33, 200MB HD, 8MB RAM, and a 15-inch or larger monitor to squeeze lots of windows onto your screen.

In This Chapter, You Learned . . .

It almost always makes sense to bolster your flagging PC with new hardware, but there may be a software solution you can try before you buy costly new goodies. If you and your PC decide to part company, check out some of the smart new upgradables. While you're at it, see just what Windows experts recommend to run the GUI for the rest of us.

Jär-gen:

What is a Windows workstation, anyway? In spite of all the hype, it's very simple. A Windows workstation is any computer that's capable of running Microsoft Windows. In most cases the systems marketed as such have extra features that make Windows run better, such as a graphics accelerator card, a large monitor, and/or a fast microprocessor.

Chapter 3 Checklist: Is Upgrading Worth the Hassle?

- What are the bottlenecks in my current system?

- What would it cost to replace the worst "offenders?"

- Would such an upgrade be cost effective when compared to buying a new system?

- What other resources can I call on? A friend with spare components? A new motherboard from a local dealer, or a used one from a PC swap meet?

- Have I considered software and small hardware "fixes" to my system's bottlenecks?

- If it's time for a new system, have I looked at upgradable PCs? Windows-configured systems?

Notes: _____

_____

_____

_____

_____

_____

Memory Upgrading

It was a dark and stormy night. Maxine bent her head against the blustery gale and trudged onward through the wet streets. "Just half a block more," she urged, trying to lift her own spirits, just as the wind had lifted the tattered umbrella out of her grasp only moments before.

A lone light reflected in the slick pavement ahead. As she neared the shabby storefront, the hand-lettered sign on the door grew clearer: *RAM-O-RAMA—Open 24 hours.*

Her heart lifted in joy. "More RAM," she cried out, heedless of the spectacle she was creating. "More RAM, please!"

What's the Big Deal with RAM?

RAM stands for *Random Access Memory*, and it's the microprocessor's holding tank for all the flotsam and debris it digs through while working in your software and performing Important Calculations. When it finds the time, the bustling microprocessor comes back to RAM and retrieves whatever data looks interesting.

Thanks to RAM, the microprocessor is able to offload its jottings temporarily, thereby easing its load and working faster. Once it's finished, you save its work to disk and shut off your PC, and all the data in RAM disappears forever. But while the CPU's working in a program, the more RAM you have, the better off you and your PC are—as long as your software can take advantage of it.

How Much RAM's Enough?

One MB of RAM equals about a million bytes, or 1,024K. The fastest PCs on the market, the 386 and 486, generally come with 2 to 8MB of RAM, but these sleek bunnies can access up to 4 billion bytes (*gigabytes*, or *GB*) of memory. If that's not enough to give you the willies, some pundits think we'll be looking at trillions of bytes (*terabytes*) before too long.

 **ISTORY**

The first PC held only 64 *kilobytes* of RAM (abbreviated *KB* or simply *K*). Today, a few PCs come with at least 640K RAM. Since most computers have more, they count their RAM capacity in *megabytes* (written *MB* or *M*).

Before you can decide how much RAM you'll need, look at your software's box, or read reviews of that software to learn how much RAM it needs to run well.

Everybody Craves RAM

If PC users have one thing in common, they all want more RAM. Well, current software, huge as it is, wants RAM even more.

- RAM helps Windows users run the larger GUI programs—several of them at once, if their PCs have enough memory. Windows runs faster, in part, because it doesn't have to scurry over to the comparatively slow hard disk every time it wants some information—some of it is already in RAM.

- DOS users, too, can use the task-switching abilities under certain user interfaces. Those users with 386 or 486 PCs can run the newer, 386-based applications with the memory these programs demand. And even those users who have only 1MB can load all their device drivers and memory-resident programs in an out-of-the-way memory area called *high memory*.

> **Jär-gen:**
>
> *High memory, upper memory, and extended memory are all areas of RAM beyond the conventional 640K that the computer uses directly. For more information about how a PC uses memory, pick up* 10 Minute Guide to Memory Management *by Jennifer Flynn.*

- Even OS/2 aficionados can benefit from extra memory. In fact, folks who want to run the OS/2 operating system shouldn't scrimp one bit on RAM. Even though IBM states that 4MB will do as a minimum amount, 6MB is more realistic—and 8MB is a better estimate. RAM is cheap, so be safe. Figure on 8MB to start for OS/2 itself, and for each DOS or Windows application you want to run concurrently, add 1MB.

How Can I Count My PC's RAM?

Count how much RAM is already on board your PC by watching the screen carefully at boot-up. The ROM-BIOS performs a memory self-test, where it throws a rapid succession of numbers onto the PC's screen. The final numbers you see represent the amount of RAM it counted.

What Kind of Chips Should I Buy?

The hardest part of upgrading your RAM just may be figuring what multiples of which size chips to buy. The most commonly seen RAM chips are DRAMs, and these come in three styles, as shown in Figure 4.1. (Check Chapter 16 for installation details.)

Figure 4.1

RAM comes in several types of packages.

DIPs

SIPs

SIMMs

- *DIPs:* This stands for *Dual In-line Package.* It's a boxy rectangular fellow with eight metal legs on either long side. You plug these legs into a special socket. (These are considered older, and may be getting harder to find. If your motherboard requires DIPs, consider upgrading to full capacity when you do find them.)

- *SIMMs:* This stands for *Single In-line Memory Modules.* This type of memory comes on a long strip, with several (usually three or nine) DIP chips fitted onto it. You press it into a special slot on the motherboard.

- *SIPs:* This stands for *Single In-line Package*, and resembles the SIMM except for the fact that it connects to the motherboard with little pins on the edge of the "card" instead of an expansion-card-like connector.

Now that you know the three types, look at your system's manuals to determine which type you need.

Unfortunately, it's not as simple as just selecting from among three packaging styles; each one comes in a variety of capacities and speeds.

- *Capacity:* Chips come in capacities ranging from 16K up to the more common 256K and 1MB sizes. Chips that hold 4MB are increasingly popular on newer systems. Consult your motherboard's manual to see what capacities your system accepts.

- *Speed:* RAM speed, measured in *nanoseconds* (*ns*), ranges from 50ns to 120ns for SIMMs. In this instance, the *lower* the number, the faster the chip's speed. (It's possible to mix speeds, but it's not a good idea. Mixing speeds can sometimes cause memory errors that are very hard to troubleshoot.)

Study your system manual carefully for RAM requirements before you spend your money. Some motherboards require all chips to be the same capacity. Others let you mix and match under certain carefully regulated conditions. Most encourage you to use the same speed for all chips.

Memory Cards

When your motherboard runs out of RAM room, consider buying a *memory expansion card*. You buy RAM chips and stick them on the card, and then stick the card into one of your expansion slots. Some brands of memory cards actually take the guesswork out of buying RAM chips. For example, Intel's Above Board memory board lets you mix SIMMS of various capacities and speeds, as long as they're slapped down on the board in pairs.

It's a good idea to fill up your motherboard's RAM slots before taking this route. Before buying a memory expansion card, make sure the card is compatible with your motherboard design, BIOS, and microprocessor.

If you're serious about wringing every last kilobyte of value out of your system's RAM, consider 386MAX or QEMM. If you're a laid-back type that doesn't care about "maximum performance" as long as the system functions, stick with DOS's memory management.

BOTTOM LINE

Software Solutions

Whatever amount of memory you have, you'll see great improvement with the addition of a memory-management program. Two such programs, Qualitas' 386MAX and Quarterdeck's QEMM, analyze your PC's available memory and put it to use in the most efficient way.

Programs like these also can hunt down and remap memory that's assigned to unused video and BIOS modes. In addition, memory managers seek out memory-resident programs and device drivers (programs that would otherwise compete for the same scant 640K memory turf), and load them into vacant corners of high memory.

With a memory management system in place, you can increase the amount of conventional RAM available to your programs by stuffing drivers and system programs into other RAM that normally sits idle. You can also set up extended or expanded memory for use by any of your application programs that are written to take advantage of it.

DOS 5 comes with the basic memory management tools to do all these things, but DOS 5's system is not quite as efficient as these third-party products (386MAX and QEMM). The third-party products are also much easier to set up than DOS's memory management system.

ISTORY

When early PC users became fed up with the PC's inherent 640K memory barrier, a few companies banded together and invented the first RAM expansion card. They called it *expanded memory,* and devised a standard to go with it called the *Expanded Memory Specification,* or *EMS.* (Since Lotus, Intel, and Microsoft were the companies who invented it, you'll see this written as LIM EMS, as well.)

When the 286 generation of PCs arrived on the scene, they contained sockets for RAM right on the motherboard. Revolutionary

continues

continued

concept! The 286's capability to house *extended memory* has carried through to the 386, and currently to the 486 (which has some newer, fancier memory managing capabilities of its own).

Okay. So far so good. Card, *expanded*; chips on motherboard, *extended*. Got it.

Here comes the strange part. Wait, don't go. In general, DOS programs don't recognize expanded or extended memory. When it's running EMS-compatible programs, DOS has to fool itself into thinking it's using expanded memory instead. Windows, OS/2, Unix and a few other operating systems understand extended memory, but they can do so only after invoking a special *enhanced mode*. (That's why Windows 3.1 was such a big to-do.)

The important thing to remember about extended and expanded memory is that your software must *recognize* one of these before you see any benefit from having it. Otherwise you'll end up with some very expensive (but mostly idle) RAM disks and print spoolers (which also use spare RAM, and are covered in Chapter 3).

In This Chapter, You Learned . . .

The first upgrade you should make is to your PC's memory, especially if you want to enjoy fully the wonders of today's software. Adding a memory manager to your arsenal will help you take advantage of this upgrade, and learn more about memory in the process.

Chapter 4 Checklist: Memory Upgrades

- How much RAM does my PC presently have?
- What is my motherboard's RAM capacity ceiling?
- What are the RAM requirements of the software I want to run?
- What will bringing my RAM up to this level cost?
- What is the speed of my RAM chips? Is this speed available from a vendor?
- What types of chips and what capacities will I need?
- Do I need a memory manager program?
- Would a memory card expand on my motherboard's RAM capacity?
- If the RAM upgrade path's too steep for me right now, would other software perform my needed tasks with less RAM required?

Notes: _____

_____

_____

_____

_____

_____

_____

_____

_____

_____

_____

_____

_____

_____

_____

_____

_____

A New Hard Drive

Time for a break. Stand straight up, arms in the air, and twist. Have a seat. Ahh, that's better. Why not take your shoes off and wiggle your toes while you're at it? Deep breath. There. You always feel better after a nice long stretch.

Your PC feels better when it has a little breathing room, too. In fact, a cramped hard disk can cause data loss and all sorts of problems. But it's easy enough to upgrade a hard disk. Almost as easy as taking a stretch!

Hard Drives

A hard disk is a much more efficient storage device than a floppy disk. For one thing, the entire disk is sealed inside a casing, where no dust particles can come between the read/write head and the disk platters. For another, the actual disk inside the casing is made of hard metal (hence the name "hard disk") rather than that floppy stuff. Figure 5.1 shows what's inside the casing.

Figure 5.1

A hard disk spins inside a sealed case, where read/write heads access it.

Hardly anyone has to be talked into a bigger hard drive. After all, who would turn down the chance for more closet space? Well, your computer can always use more space, too. Besides holding more data, the new crop of hard drives is smarter. And although they're one of the pricier PC components, the hard drive's price, per megabyte of storage, has fallen steadily through the years.

But "bigger" is not the only consideration when shopping for a hard disk. Many features affect a particular model's desirability. When shopping for a new drive, compare *all* of the following features.

Formatted Capacity

As with most PC storage options, a hard drive's capacity is measured in *megabytes* (or *MB*). A disk must be readied for use through a process known as *formatting*. Most are sold preformatted, although their capacity may still be advertised at the unformatted rate. Ask. If you buy an unformatted drive, ask what the drive's capacity will be *after* formatting.

NOTE

A good rule of thumb for estimating your hard disk needs is to add up the size (in MB) of the programs you use, and double that total to figure in your data. Then double that figure to allow for growth (and that neat new graphics program you've been eyeing). Another method, perhaps not as precise, is to take the biggest drive you can afford and squeak past it one notch for good measure.

Speed

Hard drive speeds are measured in *milliseconds* (*ms*) of average data access time, and range from around 13ms (fast) to more than 25ms (snail-mode). You also need to look at the drive's *data transfer rate*, ranging from around 700K per second (fast) to 500K per second (slow). Obviously, look for the fastest drive you can afford.

MTBF

This melodious acronym stands for *Mean Time Between Failures*, measured in the number of hours a drive should rack up before it fails. If a drive has an MTBF of 25,000, they're betting on it to keep chugging away for 25,000 hours before it dies. Look for an MTBF of 20,000 or more, but the hard drive makers set these numbers, so be cautious.

Casing Size

Drives come in *full-height* and *half-height* formats (to fit full-height and half-height drive bays) and several sizes, all the way down to 1.3-inch models. Today's PCs favor the smaller-format, half-height bays. Assess the number and sizes of drive bays inside your PC's case before you shop.

If you're buying a second hard drive, make sure it's compatible with your existing controller card. You'll need a second cable as well.

BOTTOM LINE

Controllers

A hard drive uses a *controller* to direct data access. The controller technology determines the drive's type. Some controllers come built into the drive; others come on expansion cards to put inside your PC. A hard disk controller commonly contains a floppy drive controller, too. The dealer will help you select the right controller for your new hard drive.

A *cache controller* reduces the (often slow) data transfer process by storing oft-used data in a *memory buffer*. If data there needs to be accessed once again, the cache sends it to the CPU, leaving the slower hard disk access out of the loop. Cache software is also available, discussed further in Chapter 3.

Drive Type

Drive type is closely related to the controller, since the drive type you purchase will determine the controller you need. Here's a summary of the popular drive types:

Hard disk cache controllers are expensive ($500 to $2,000), and work well only in applications that need to check out your hard disk frequently. Be sure to evaluate a software cache solution before you decide on this option.

BOTTOM LINE

NOTE

The term "drive type" can mean two different things. It refers to the basic type of drive, as discussed in this section, but also to a type number, such as 32 or 48. The drive type number, usually written on the casing, is important when you are setting up the drive.

- *IDE* stands for Intelligent Drive Electronics and represents another way of stretching the AT expansion bus: the controller sits right on the drive itself. The drive is mostly self-controlled, offloading the traditional CPU tasks of low-level disk control functions.

- *ESDI*, or Enhanced Small Device Interface, is the current high-end, high-capacity drive controller in favor. ESDI offers high speed and high capacity on a card.

- *SCSI* is Small Computer System Interface and connects everything from CD-ROMs to tape drives and hard disks. The SCSI controller's more commonly called a *host adapter*, and once inside your PC's expansion bus, one card can control up to seven drives or other devices (actually, it's eight; the PC itself counts as one). Be sure to read the SCSI section in Chapter 8 to learn more.

Hard Cards

If you're running out of hard disk space, you don't necessarily have to buy a full-fledged new hard disk.

A faster and more convenient solution exists: *hard cards*. A hard card is just that: a hard disk on an expansion card. Hard cards come very close to hard disks in speed and performance. Plus, you don't have to worry about matching the proper controller (if it's not part of the drive) with the proper hard disk. If you need an easy solution and don't mind paying the higher price, a hard card may be for you. Be sure to compare this option when you're shopping.

> *Another option is disk compression software, such as Stacker. This special software or software/expansion card combination tricks your PC into storing about twice as much information on your existing hard disk as would normally fit. See Chapter 3 for other software tricks to improve your hard disk's performance.*

In This Chapter, You Learned . . .

How does the old saying go—"You can never be too rich, too thin, or have too big a hard drive." Expanding your disk storage is an easy and dramatic way to upgrade your PC. And with prices for storage so low, there's never been a better time.

When selecting a hard drive, balance your needs for mass quantities of storage against a drive's speed and reliability. Make sure that you have (or can get) the right kind of controller, too.

Chapter 5 Checklist: A New Hard Drive

- What is my current hard drive interface, speed, and capacity?

  Interface   Speed   Capacity

  _____   _____   _____

- What are my storage needs?
- Must I remain compatible with a certain interface?
- Have I looked at IDE drives?
- Would my assortment of peripherals suggest looking at a SCSI hard drive?

Notes: _____

_____

_____

_____

_____

Versatile Storage

The digital readout blinked midnight as Lou slid another floppy disk into the drive and typed **Format C:**. Mindlessly, almost numbly, he typed **Y** in response to the PC's robotic **Proceed with format?**

Only one more floppy and the yearly report would be finished and backed up—not a moment too soon to meet tomorrow's deadline, Lou mused dreamily. Suddenly, the hard drive whirred and the screen blanked. Lou had just reformatted his hard disk, sending a day's work to Bit Heaven. Not a good time to mistake a **C:** for a **B:**!

Lou was fortunate. He'd been pretty good about backing the day's work to floppies each night. Even so, restoring his hard disk from the floppy disks would take hours. And the work he'd accomplished today was gone for good.

Protecting your data against loss used to mean backing it up to floppies. Today, a host of storage solutions can automate the process—saving you time and grief. And it probably won't surprise you to learn that floppy drives themselves have improved.

Adding Another Floppy Drive

Maybe you want to avoid the hassle of swapping low-capacity floppies all day long, or perhaps you just want to become compatible with your laptop's 3 1/2-inch drive. As disks hold more and become smaller, sooner or later you'll be upgrading your floppy drive.

Buying a Floppy Drive

For years, people have been forced to stick two disk drives in their PCs, a 3 1/2-inch and a 5 1/4-inch model. A sleek dual-diskette drive by TEAC offers both sizes in one half-height unit. (Check out Figure 6.1.) This solution saves on space and on the hassle of connecting cables and controllers, since both drives work off the same power and controller connections. Buy one of these and you can remove the old single-sized drive and have room for a CD-ROM. Now *that's* an upgrade!

Or you may opt for one of the standard single-drive units pictured in Figure 6.2:

- A 3 1/2-inch high-density drive, with 1.4MB capacity.
- A 3 1/2-inch low-density drive, with 720K capacity.
- A 5 1/4-inch high-density drive, with 1.2MB capacity.

Since you're upgrading, you're probably not interested in another 5 1/4-inch low-density drive with a 360K capacity (pictured in Figure 6.2).

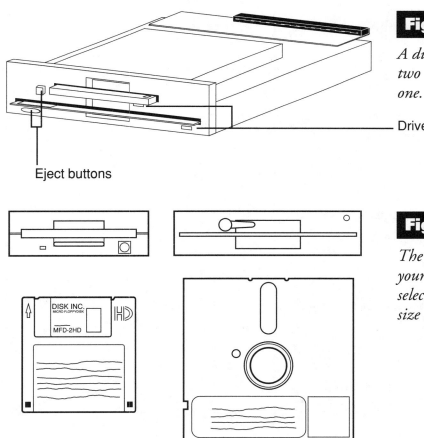

Figure 6.1

A dual-diskette drive crams two drives into the space of one.

Drive access lights

Eject buttons

Figure 6.2

The first step in upgrading your floppy drives is to select the optimum drive size and capacity.

DISK INC.
MICRO FLOPPYDISK
MFD-2HD
HD

Whatever model you buy, you'll need a drive unit, a controller card, and a cable.

Floppy drives are mounted on drive bays in the system unit. For more details on installation, turn to the "Installing a Disk Drive" section of Chapter 16. After you slide in the drive, one of the new floppy drives will need to be designated as the *boot drive*. You'll choose a drive to be either Drive A: or Drive B: by the way you hook up its cable to the controller. Another connector links the drive to the PC's power supply. Follow the manual and be sure to set any jumpers or DIP switches necessary for your PC's configuration.

NOTE

One way you shouldn't "upgrade" your computer is by listening to people who say you can punch a hole in a low-capacity (low-density) 3 1/2 inch disk in order to turn it into a high-capacity (high-density) disk. After all, that extra hole in the corner of the high-capacity floppy looks to be the only difference between the two, right? WRONG. The two types of disks differ internally, and while the trick may work, it won't be reliable. And neither will your data's safety.

Tape to Ease Backing Up

Apart from automating the daily backup process, tape drives are a great solution for those who need to archive important but "dusty" data. Data security is another popular reason to back up, but if security procedures (including backing up) are too cumbersome, you just won't follow them.

Imagine yourself backing up and lugging home a clumsy pile of floppies each night. Hardly! Now picture yourself with a single tape cartridge shoved into your coat pocket. If the office building burns down in the night, the next day you have your client list or billings, all the same. Tape backup systems provide an easy way to copy huge, unwieldy files—and mail them across the country, too! (To be on the safe side, mark these parcels MAGNETIC MEDIA—DO NOT X-RAY.)

Many other backup solutions vie for your backup buck, but the most inexpensive, upgradable solution is still tape.

- Before you buy, consider which files you'll back up daily, and which ones need backing up less frequently. Figure the capacity you need based on the maximum amount of data you'll back up in one session. Ideally, you'll want your unit to hold at least one hard disk partition's work, and preferably the contents of your entire hard disk. But it really depends on you and your backup needs.

- Remember, data on tape is *sequentially accessed*, and can be more difficult to find than data on a randomly-accessed medium like a floppy disk.

- Try out different brands before you buy, if possible, to make sure you like the software. Make sure you get automated backups, macros, batch files, and the ability to run under Windows or other operating systems you use.

- What's the true data capacity of the unit? Some brands advertise a capacity that's for compressed data only.

- Check for compatibility in recording formats: you'll want a unit that follows recording standards. Also, make sure the vendor will be around in a few years to supply your next level of storage capacity; switching brands can mean risking data-conversion hassles.

Flopticals

Just pronouncing it makes you want to turn around and look for Allen Funt behind the candid camera. (Those storage people have such a great sense of humor!) Floptical drives fit into the standard 3 1/2-inch drive bay. The drives can read from and write to standard 720K and 1.44MB diskettes, as well as jumbo floptical disks holding more than 20MB of data. They're faster than standard floppy drives—a floptical's average access time is around 120 milliseconds (ms). Capacity and performance come at a price: The drives run about $500, while the disks go for $22 each.

Bernoulli Drives

In a hybrid twist on hard disk technology (a combo hard disk and floppy), *Bernoulli drives* hover over the read/write head. Unlike a hard disk, the Bernoulli's high-density disks are removable. They cost about $800, hold about 90MB of data, and their average access time is 28ms. They have an advantage over tape because their data's randomly accessible. The drive looks like another hard drive to your PC, so you can access whatever files you want just by listing a directory and pulling a file.

Magneto-Optical Drives

If you can picture storing data on a compact disk, you can picture a magneto-optical drive. Slow and expensive, current magneto-optical drives run about $2,000 and take 47ms to access data—sluggish when compared to a typical hard drive's 22ms. The bottom line is to wait for this technology to mature some.

In This Chapter You Learned . . .

Upgrading your PC's floppy drives isn't exactly the most common upgrade ever performed. Yet, a floppy drive is touched and accessed many times throughout your computing sessions, and if it's the wrong size or otherwise inconvenient, it's a non-optimal component that should be changed.

If your high-capacity hard drive or security-sensitive data needs better backup procedures, look at one of the tape drives, flopticals, Bernoullis, or other solutions crowding the mail-order catalogs and computer store shelves.

Chapter 6 Checklist: Storage Solutions

- Would my intended software load faster with a new floppy drive?

- Do I need a particular sized floppy drive so I can be compatible with the PC at work? A friend's? A laptop?

- Have I looked at the dual-drive model?

- Would my requirements ever include a tape-backup unit?

- Is this compatible with other units I'd be working with?

- Would another storage solution provide enhanced performance? Is this worth the higher price?

Notes: _____

_____

_____

_____

_____

Updating the CPU and Motherboard

It may seem a drastic measure, but dramatic performance gains are yours if you dare. . . All you have to do to get them is be willing to fondle and poke mega-hundred-dollar chips—or to remove every component in your system box and replace each one, in order, on top of a new motherboard. Piece of cake! Ready?

Upgrading the CPU

In general, applications that require a fast CPU also require a fast system bus, video subsystem, and hard disk. That's why there are few straight chip upgrades available. Unfortunately, the best way to get a new chip is a hassle, too: replacing the motherboard. (That's especially true with the DX2, or Overdrive, line of chips, which don't perform to their full potential without a secondary RAM cache.)

Performance Gains from Chip Upgrades

Each level of microprocessor can benefit you. Check out Table 7.1 to see what specific gains you'll see from that gleaming new chip.

Table 7.1 Each chip offers improvements over its predecessor.

From	*To*	*Leads to These Performance Upgrade(s):*
286	386SX	Better memory management, and multitasking under Windows or DESQview.
386SX	386DX	Full-fledged 32-bit data paths will double the data transfer, and do it faster.
386DX	486SX	Internal 8K cache keeps oft-used data at the fore; provides higher performance.
486SX	486	Math coprocessor onboard; higher clock speeds available (top-dog status).
486	486DX2	Under ideal conditions, doubles internal clock speed (e.g., a 25MHz chip to 50MHz speeds).

A few vendors sell a chip-replacement module that boosts a 286's performance to that of a 386SX. This is accomplished by removing your 286 chip with a special chip-removal tool (included in most product packages), and inserting a circuit board that replaces the 286 chip. Software is included that updates your system files. Intel makes a product called SnapIn 386, but they claim it will only work with True Blue IBM PCs. It's costly, and your software only runs 1.5 to 2 times faster. Kingston Technologies makes a similar product, and although it's been used successfully with clones, they only guarantee and support installations in Compaqs, IBMs and some other high-end brands. Other brands of processor upgrade modules undoubtedly exist, but you should research performance gains vs. cost.

Owners of 486 systems who want to upgrade can buy special Over-drive chips that accelerate the chip's internal instruction processing to twice the system board's clock speed. You can remove your 486DX/25 from its socket and insert a 486DX2/25, for example, to gain 50MHz performance rates under limited conditions.

Accelerator boards offer chips (and often system memory) on an expansion card. This is not the best way to upgrade your chip, because you'll only see full performance benefits if you have an MCA or EISA expansion bus, which allows the board a better connection with the rest of the system. (It's improbable that many people are upgrading EISAs, which are relatively recent PCs.)

Adding a Math Coprocessor

A *math coprocessor* is a chip that speeds the CPU's ability to do a certain type of mathematical work, involving fractions called *floating-point operations.* The math coprocessor adds about 70 extra numeric functions that tackle the math stuff, boosting performance for these specific operations by up to 500 percent.

Numeric operations aren't limited to financial calculations and math. If you do vector-oriented graphics, design (or use) many fonts, or design and test structures using *computer-aided design* (*CAD*), you'll see improvements in speed when you add a math coprocessor. Of course, the applications you'd think would benefit from a math coprocessor, do: namely, spreadsheets, statistical analysis programs, and databases.

Remember these key points when adding a math coprocessor to your system.

- Your software must be able to work with the math coprocessor in order for it to do any good.

- For each microprocessor there's a corresponding math coprocessor, as shown in Table 7.2.

Table 7.2   Buy the right math coprocessor for your system.

Microprocessor	Math Coprocessor
486DX	Already built into 486DX
486SX*	487SX*
386SX/33MHz	387DX-33
386SX/25	387DX-25
386DX/20	387DX-20
386DX/16	387DX-16
386SX/20	387SX-20
386SX/16	387SX-16
286	80287 XL
8088 or 8086 10MHz	8087-1
8088 or 8086 8MHz	8087-2
8088 or 8086 4MHz	8087-3

*People found that adding the cost of a math coprocessor with the cost of the 486SX system totaled more than buying a full-fledged 486DX PC in the first place. So the 487SX qualified as one of chip-maker Intel Corp.'s biggest marketing disasters of all time. Intel is currently urging users to fill the vacant 487SX slot on their motherboards with an Overdrive chip instead.

In addition to the chips in Table 7.2, Intel Corp. markets RapidCAD, a coprocessor targeted specifically to engineering applications.

Installing the Coprocessor

To install a coprocessor, you need to turn off your PC and all peripherals, unplug everything, remove the lid, tap the unpainted metal framework to ground yourself, and locate the vacant coprocessor socket. Carefully, take the chip in hand, oriented with the chip's notched corner to the notch on its destined socket, and press it gently into place. Now press a little more firmly. Voilà!

You'll want to tell your PC (whatever model you own) about the new intruder. You do this by setting the proper DIP switches (on an XT), or running the setup program (on an AT) to see if the AT has recognized the math coprocessor automatically. You might have to reconfigure your software, too, to get it to work with the new chip.

A New Motherboard

Put simply, a new motherboard can provide you with the framework of a new PC, as shown in Figure 7.1. Specifically, you'll benefit from the expanded system bus width and the extra RAM sockets, not to mention the new motherboard's capacity for a coprocessor and other add-ons. Best of all, most computer gurus consider adding a new motherboard just a simple "open the case, unplug everything, take out the old, put in the new, plug everything in again and close up the case" (breathe here) operation. (Sorry, these guys *don't* make house calls!)

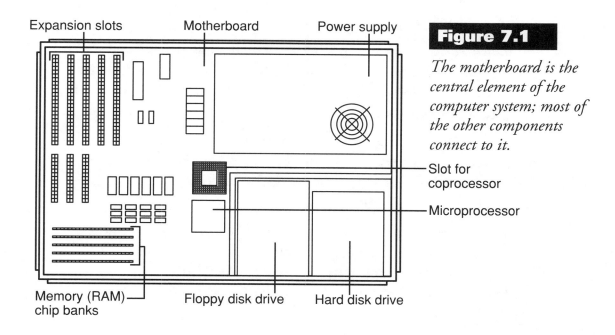

Expansion slots   Motherboard   Power supply

Slot for coprocessor

Microprocessor

Memory (RAM) chip banks   Floppy disk drive   Hard disk drive

Figure 7.1

The motherboard is the central element of the computer system; most of the other components connect to it.

Every motherboard upgrade isn't guaranteed to go as smoothly as this. Keep in mind the following factors when shopping:

- *Size:* Before you buy, make sure the motherboard will fit inside your system box.

- *Microprocessor:* Verify you're getting the chip you want on the new motherboard.

- *Documentation:* You'll need a thorough, well-written manual for the new motherboard, to learn what RAM chip configurations you can use, as well as the location of ROM chips, DIP switches, and other essentials.

After you've purchased the new motherboard, you'll want to exercise every precaution to ensure that it goes from the package to your system without being stepped on, fried by static electricity, bent, folded, stapled, or mutilated. Here are some tips:

- If you need a large, clear working surface for most upgrades, you'll need the largest, clearest working surface for this one, since *everything*—every component and every RAM chip in the system box—will need to come out and hang around on your desk or table.

- You'll need to turn off the computer and all components, unplug everything and take everything out of the system box. (As you know, the motherboard is underneath the other parts. See Figure 7.2.) Before you remove the components it's a good idea to connect masking tape labels to the connectors and cables, labeling the position of each. And don't worry about residual electrical charges; this isn't your old audio tape deck.

• It wouldn't hurt to grab some large sheets of butcher paper and draw a nearly-scale template of the motherboard's layout. As you remove labeled components, plop them down on their approximate locations on the template. This ensures a (relatively) care-free reassembly.

• As you remove screws from the old board, keep them in a small cup on your working surface. Slide out the old motherboard, then slide the new one into the space and reconnect the cables.

• *Be careful how you plug in the power supply.* I cannot overstress this point. It is possible to plug in the power connectors of the motherboard *backwards.* Doing so will damage your entire new motherboard (and possibly damage you). The power supply shoots power to the motherboard via a single long connector, or two multi-wire connectors. Before you disconnect the connector(s), examine them carefully. You must reinstall them properly, and not try to jam them on backwards.

Figure 7.2

Once all the connectors have been removed, the motherboard slides out of its frame easily.

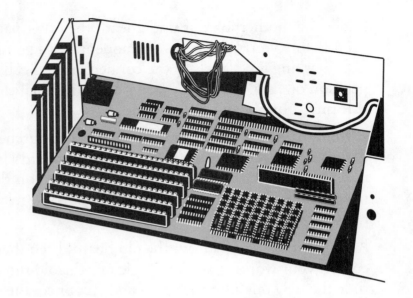

NOTE

If you've upgraded your XT's motherboard to a 386 or better, determine your power supply's wattage. If it's the old XT's 135-watt model, you'll need to upgrade to a 200-watt power supply, or your new motherboard won't be supported.

These tips give you a place to start, but don't rely on them as instructions; use the documentation that comes with the new motherboard as your guide, referring to the original system documentation as needed.

Sometimes you must upgrade your PC before you can perform the more essential upgrades to your system. Keep reading to see when you should update your ROM BIOS chip(s).

Replacing Your ROM BIOS

The PC is very impressionable. And it's the ROM BIOS, housed in one or more chips on the motherboard, which stamps its own personality on the PC. The *ROM* part stands for *Read-Only Memory*, a permanent set of instructions etched onto the ROM chip. Part of these instructions are the PC's *BIOS* (which stands for *Basic Input-Output System*). In a lightning-fast series of system checks and verifications, the BIOS *initializes* the PC at boot-up, and assists the CPU in other ways.

Personal computer hardware advances rapidly (as you know all too well, since that's the reason you need to upgrade)! But the ROM BIOS (unlike other forms of memory) can't be written to. Yet a PC's ROM BIOS is in charge of checking on many of the hardware components at initialization; it can't afford to be outdated, or it won't be able to recognize and work with many of the new controllers and other gizmos. What to do? Don't despair. If your ROM has fallen behind the times, you can upgrade it.

Installing ROM Chips

First thing: Turn off your PC and unplug everything, before you even *read* the following section!

ROM chips are available by mail order, or some local dealers may stock them. The important thing is to get written instructions for both the ROM chips *and* your motherboard before you start. Motherboards vary, so you'll need to dig up (and have handy) the manual for yours to learn where the ROM chips are housed, and how many you'll need. The new ROM chips should come with documentation, as well as telephone technical support (preferably toll-free).

NOTE

This is actually a great time to invite the PC guru from work over for some rousing computer-game fun and a motherboard overhaul. Chinese food makes great bait. (The guru will probably enjoy "hacking" the motherboard more than blasting the trolls and munching the wontons!)

Do not attempt to install ROM chips without clear, illustrated documentation. Have I warned you enough? The reason you need illustrated, clearly written documentation before you change ROM chips is to *make sure you don't insert them backwards.* Otherwise you will fry the chips and your motherboard; quite possibly, your whole house will explode (well, okay, maybe not, but it wouldn't hurt to be *that careful*).

ISTORY

It used to be that a PC was stuck with the ROM chips it came with—unless these were physically removed and new ones stuck in their place. After all, ROM stands for read-only memory, which means you can't write new instructions to it, right? Right—sort of. A fairly recent technology called *flash ROM* enables ROM updates through software that effectively erases and reprograms the ROM chips. Alas, only those people who have flash ROM chips already installed on their motherboards can upgrade their ROM in this way.

In This Chapter, You Learned. . .

Although these upgrades are a little more trouble than most, nothing changes the nature of your PC more effectively than a new micropro-cessor, math chip, motherboard, or ROM chipset. Since the new components are costly and fragile, you'll need to proceed carefully, with full documentation (and a techie friend) at hand.

Chapter 7 Checklist: Adding a New CPU

- What class of CPU does my PC have now?
- What CPU does my targeted software require?
- Does my software support (and would it improve with) a math coprocessor?
- Does my motherboard have a slot for a math coprocessor?
- Would future upgrades go more smoothly if I changed my ROM BIOS?
- Have I considered replacing my system's motherboard?

Notes: _____

_____

_____

_____

_____

_____

_____

_____

_____

_____

_____

_____

_____

_____

_____

_____

_____

_____

_____

_____

_____

_____

More Ports, Please!

Olga searched frantically for her PC's manual. She was sure she'd never before seen that strange word: *SCSI*. Darn! She couldn't find a word about it, yet the CD-ROM drive that Mom gave her for her birthday needed something called a SCSI interface.

Olga needn't panic. Adding ports to a PC is one of the most common (and easiest) upgrades. (Getting everything to work with the more temperamental SCSI adapters is another story, but one that's told here, too.)

Adding New Ports to a PC

You can give your PC new life (well, room for more serial and parallel devices, anyway) by purchasing a serial or parallel port card. Or you can opt for a *multifunction* card, which holds an assortment of new ports—typically two serial and one parallel, plus a game port for a joystick. Although the upgrade itself involves little more than inserting another expansion card into one of your PC's free slots, you'll need to keep the following in mind:

- *Will the card fit?* Expansion cards come tall, short, fat, and thin. Before you buy a new card, make sure you know the dimensions of your PC's case. Warning: you may have to rearrange the other cards inside the system box to make the newcomer nice and comfy. (Think of it as *practice!*)

- *The ports and devices must match.* The type of port card you add to your PC depends on the type of new device you want to hook up. You'll need a serial port for a serial modem, a parallel port for a parallel printer, and so on. A multifunction card offers both types, so you don't have to worry as much.

- *Switches, jumpers, and bears, oh my!* Expansion cards sport tiny switches and things called jumpers that you may be called upon to manipulate in some way. The manual will tell you how to set them to achieve various configurations on your PC and new port.

  Switches are nice and familiar. You've seen light switches before, so imagine the smallest possible light switch—on and off. That's it! Jumpers can be likened to bridges that sit atop pilings, only the pilings are tiny pins. The jumpers can connect two pins horizontally, or you can move the jumper to connect the pins vertically instead, as shown in Figure 8.1.

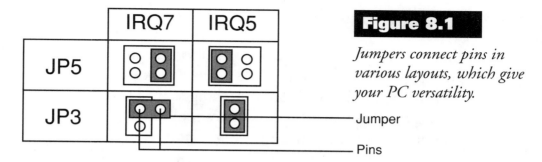

Figure 8.1

Jumpers connect pins in various layouts, which give your PC versatility.

- *Contention:* Some motherboards can't handle conflict and just send everyone to bed without any supper. If any two ports, cards, or devices clamor for the PC's attention in the same spot, the PC throws up its hands (not a pretty sight!) in disgust. Think carefully about the devices you already have and what new ones you're adding. Be sure to set jumpers and DIP switches carefully, and use the chart at the end of this chapter to determine vacant playground turf. (If you added another serial port and now you have none, that's contention. You'll need to set switches on the new serial port to let the newcomer know its turn is next.)

- *Connectors:* Place your new card carefully on the motherboard, taking into account any connector cables that may need extra room.

Game Ports

The original game port was designed for the anemic first IBM PC/XT, not the powerhouses of today. Since the dark suits at IBM never bothered to update the specs on something as un-businesslike as a game port, the joystick makers themselves took up the slack. If you're having trouble with your joystick on a high-speed computer, look for the replacement game cards by joystick makers like Advanced Gravis and Kraft. These hopped-up models have a special knob right on the card that lets you match the card's data rate with your computer's speed. (And zap Gir Draxon once for me, while you're at it.)

SCSI Time

Question: When is a port more than a port? When it's a SCSI port. SCSI's short for *Small Computer System Interface*. Like a PC's other ports, a SCSI port links external devices like printers or CD-ROM drives to the expansion bus. That's where the similarity ends.

Jär-gen:

Whether expansion bus or just plain bus, it's the same: the system of expansion slots on a PC's motherboard where you can add neat goodies.

The ultra-fast SCSI *host adapter* offers a connection between your PC and as many as seven other SCSI devices (the PC/host adapter together count as one device). These link to each other in a "daisy-chain" fashion and are able to run simultaneously.

SCSI's more like a bus itself, effectively multiplying the number of expansion slots in your PC. As increasing numbers of SCSI drives, printers, and other devices appear, SCSI's an optimal solution for those upgraders who own small-footprint PCs that proffer few expansion slots.

The Downside to SCSI

Sounds great? All is not roses with SCSI. Until very recently, SCSI standards were askew, resulting in a motley crop of device drivers and interface cards. A new specification, SCSI-2 (Son of SCSI?), is breaking through the fracas, and soon a universally recognized SCSI-2 command set will reign triumphant.

Until SCSI-2 implements truth, justice, and the SCSI way, however, existing hosts and devices continue to run amok. SCSI's nonstandard nature shouldn't concern you if you only need to connect a single device. It's when you try to link more than a couple that all hell breaks loose.

The Lazy Path to SCSI

Some PC gurus recommend avoiding the whole SCSI mess by purchasing a separate SCSI host adapter for each SCSI device you buy. No way! Who needs the extra expense? And who wants to give up all their spare expansion slots to house all those host adapter cards? Besides, contention and conflicts are frequent enough with PCs without adding fuel to the fire.

Unfortunately, right now there's no easy path to SCSI. Take it slow and be methodical. And write down everything you do.

NOTE

Write down each step you take while installing your SCSI adapter and devices. That way, if you encounter any problems, you can unravel the SCSI chaos thread by thread.

Buying a SCSI Host Adapter

One of the best ways to avoid problems is to consider your SCSI purchase wisely. These guidelines can help it all make sense.

- *Speed:* Look for a 16-bit SCSI host adapter to enable faster data transfer between device and motherboard.

- *Compatibility:* Before you buy, find out as much as you can about the SCSI adapter's compatibility with other brands of SCSI devices. (Save your research notes. You may need them later as ammunition against over-optimistic vendors.)

- *Cache ability:* Determine how you'll use your SCSI adapter. If you often need to access the same database off a hard disk, or off a slower device (like a CD-ROM drive), you may benefit from a more expensive SCSI adapter equipped with a data cache. Note that caching only works well with oft-accessed data.

> **Jär-gen:**
>
> *A data cache holds oft-used info so your CPU can fetch it more quickly by avoiding the usual rooting around on the disk for it. Some extra-smart caches even predict what your CPU needs next!*

- *Full device addressing:* Check to be sure the SCSI adapter actually can host seven SCSI devices—if you think you'll make use of the additional expansion room (you will). Remember: the PC and host adapter each count as one device. Some of the addresses may be disabled by the manufacturer, so check on this.

- *Cables:* Since SCSI devices connect in a daisy-chain arrangement, you'll need plenty of cables. Count on at least one 25-pin to 36-pin cable to run from the adapter to the first device. As your daisy chain grows, you'll need to remember to buy additional cables, plus internal connectors for internal SCSI devices. Be sure to count the pins on the devices as well as on the cables.

Ports in a Storm

The CPU endeavors to teach some manners to the rowdy devices clamoring for its attention. It does this by assigning each one something called an *interrupt*. Interrupts let the device catch the PC's attention (by "asking nice," you could say) to make the PC do its bidding. You can press the "**Y**" on your keyboard, for example, which sends an *interrupt request* (or *IRQ*) to your PC. The PC stops what it was doing, and slaps a Y up on the monitor. Each card or port has its own unique interrupt, expressed in a number. Although two devices can share an interrupt, only one can be in use at a time—when they're behaving nicely.

Sometimes a PC experiences *interrupt conflicts*—mainly when two devices break the rules and go for the same interrupt, confusing the poor PC. The installation process should tell your PC how to assign an interrupt for your new port. If you get an interrupt conflict anyway, you'll need to know how to assign an interrupt manually. (Don't worry, you don't have to slap the device and risk imprisonment for device-abuse.) Set the interrupt by moving jumpers or switches on the new card. If you have an AT, you can use any vacant interrupt between 3 and 15. Those of you upgrading your XTs can use interrupts 2 through 7, if they're free.

To find out which interrupts are free, use a diagnostic utility program. Popular diagnostic software includes The Norton Utilities and

Quarterdeck's Manifest. As an alternative (since system components are usually assigned standard interrupts), you could use Table 8.1 to narrow down your free interrupts by a process of elimination:

Table 8.1   AT (286 and 386) standard interrupt assignments (note XT interrupts in italics).

Interrupt Number	AT-Standard Device Assigned
3	Serial Port #2 (COM2:)
4	Serial Port #1 (COM1:)
5	Printer Port #2 (LPT2:)
6	Floppy controller
7	Printer Port #1 (LPT1:)
9	Math coprocessor
14	Hard drive controller
2	*XT-math coprocessor*
5	*XT hard disk*

Chapter 8 Checklist: More Ports for my PC

- What PC add-ons am I considering?
- What type of I/O interface, or port, do they require?

Device   Type of Port

_____   _____

_____   _____

_____   _____

_____   _____

- What ports does my PC currently offer?
- What types of ports will I require?
- Will a multifunction card do the job?
- Should I consider a SCSI interface?
- Will the port's expansion card fit into my PC's case?
- Would a game port boost my productivity? My popularity? My agility?
- Do I need any special cables?

Notes:_____

_____

_____

_____

_____

_____

_____

_____

_____

_____

_____

_____

_____

_____

_____

_____

_____

_____

_____

Get the Picture

Nothing signals "upgrade" more brightly than a new monitor and video card. Since these two team up to make a PC's display, keep reading for tips on both. Here, too, you'll learn about the pleasures of scanners and still video imaging units.

Top Dog Video Standards

Most books that teach you how to buy a PC include the inevitable litany of the history of video standards. In brief, monitors and video cards have cha-cha-cha'd through the years from crisp, no-graphics monochrome (MDA), through monochrome graphics (HGC), backwards into fuzzy color graphics (CGA), up to crisper color graphics (EGA), to today's cool standard, VGA, short for Video Graphics Array.

VGA and its rich nephew, Super VGA, are the focus of this book's video section. (After all, the subtitle says *Upgrade*, right?) These days, buying anything less than VGA will lead you down the dreaded path of computer obsolescence (the reason you're upgrading in the first place!). If you pine for a trip down monitor lane, consult the video roll call in *The Most PC for Your Money*, this book's sibling. Hurry back. (While you're gone, we'll walk slowly and gawk at the pulsating VGA graphics.)

Video Cards

It takes a *video card* to turn a monitor into anything but a blank TV screen. A video card fits in your PC's expansion slot and sports a video socket where your monitor connects. Think of a video card as a conduit for instructions between your PC and a monitor. A video card installs like any expansion card, and monitors are pretty much "plug and play." (Turn to Chapter 16 for a refresher on inserting expansion cards.)

When upgrading to VGA or SVGA, keep these comparison points in mind.

- *Resolution:* The amount of resolution on a video card determines the image sharpness of a PC's display. Resolution is expressed in numbers of *pixels*, tiny points of light that the monitor/video card can display across and down. The higher the numbers, the better the picture. VGA offers a resolution of 640 by 480 pixels; the next highest standard, Super VGA, can show 800 by 600 pixels (under some conditions, up to 1,024 by 1,280).

- *Color:* The tradeoff in PC graphics is resolution against color—the crisper the image, the fewer colors you see. Note that high-end cards offer amazing, lifelike realms of color, but you'll pay anywhere from $1,500 to $5,000 to groove on them. (Professionals and Deadheads only need apply!)

Table 9.1 shows typical levels of simultaneous color display, in bits per pixel.

> **Jär-gen:**
>
> *A video card generally offers a maximum range of colors, called a palette, but the number of colors you can see at once on the screen hardly ever approaches the much-touted palette.*

Table 9.1   Video cards support four levels of color.

Bits per pixel	Simultaneous Colors
4-bit cards	16 colors
8-bit cards	256 colors
16-bit cards (High Color)	32,768 to 65,536 colors
24-bit cards (True Color)	16.7 million colors

- *Memory:* The more memory on a video card, the higher the number of colors and maximum resolution it can display. Ask how much memory a card has when shipped and how much you can add to it later. Table 9.2. shows what you can expect at various levels of memory.

Table 9.2 Approximate performance depending on video card memory.

Video Card Memory	Resolution	Colors
256K	640 x 480	16
	800 x 600	16
512K	640 x 480	256
	800 x 600	256
	1,024 x 768	16
1MB	1,024 x 768	256
	1,280 x 1,024	16

Jär-gen:

VGA pass-through connectors link to non-VGA, coprocessed, graphics accelerators (like true-color boards) and give them VGA capabilities.

- *Software drivers:* Resolution, color—none of these performance claims mean a thing unless your software supports them through mini-programs called *software drivers*. Video cards should come with a software disk containing diagnostics, utilities, demo programs, and drivers for popular software. Video card makers frequently update drivers or add new ones. Electronic bulletin board systems (or on-line services like CompuServe) often receive the latest drivers, hot from the programmers' hands.

- *VESA compatibility:* Look for a card that's compatible with the video standards consortium, VESA. A VESA-compliant card should offer VGA pass-through connectors. You can attach additional graphics peripherals to these connectors (true-color video cards, for example).

- *Flicker:* Your video card and monitor can team up to give you a powerful headache unless you look for a high *vertical scan rate*, measured in Hertz and also known as the *refresh rate*. A video board should achieve at least a 72Hz refresh rate in your software.

- *Bus width:* Your motherboard's likely to have 8-bit and 16-bit expansion slots (and perhaps one or more 32-bit slots, if it's a 386 PC). Video cards, too, come in 8-bit, 16-bit and even 32-bit strengths. Data moves through the wider, 16-bit slots faster than through the smaller slots, just as water flows through a garden hose faster than through a straw. Filling one of your PC's wider slots with a wider video card can double the performance.

It pays to buy a name-brand video card because it's easier to get Super VGA drivers for it. For example, ZSoft's PC Paintbrush program (DOS version) provides its own Super VGA drivers for many popular video cards, but no-name cards often won't work with any of them.

BOTTOM LINE

Three Main Types of Video Cards

As you discovered in Chapter 3, the MCA, ISA, and EISA motherboard standards guarantee PC shoppers a range of price and performance. Remember which one your PC has, because you'll need to buy
a video card that's compatible with your motherboard. (Although ISA
cards fit in EISA slots, you won't benefit from EISA's 32-bit data
throughput (that is, flow) unless you select an EISA card.)

To compound your troubles, a range of video cards exists to fit in
each type of motherboard:

- *Frame buffers*—average, plain-vanilla VGA cards—give your PC a
  holding tank for processed video images, but little more. Although
  these cards can be enhanced with video memory chips, they do
  nothing to lift the burden of graphics processing from the main
  CPU. The cheaper VGA or SVGA cards (or those that sport the
  Tseng Labs ET-4000 controller) are frame buffers—the best
  choice for DOS applications and moderate graphics. Look to the
  next two on the list if you want to see VGA really rip.

- *Video accelerator cards* process certain instructions locally, sending
  the ones they can't handle to the main CPU. Video accelerator
  cards are equipped with Mach10, Weitek W5086, or S^3 accelerator
  chips and cost about $200–$350. These VGA or SVGA cards are
  also known as "Windows accelerators." Although they make
  Windows programs fly, S^3 cards can actually slow down DOS
  applications.

- *Co-processed video cards* grab the entire burden of graphics processing—doing away with the need to send video data down the molasses-bog of a data bus to the CPU, and freeing up the CPU for other functions. These SVGA cards do their best work under the 32-bit EISA standard, which costs more. Often driven by coprocessors from the Texas Instruments 34010 family, their performance comes at a price geared towards graphics diehards or professionals, generally from $1,000–$3,000. (That's *a lot* of Flying Toasters!)

Local Bus Technology

As you know, each motherboard standard presents a different PC philosophy (and certain buyer confusion!). The most recent motherboard design, *local bus*, clearly has the heavy graphics user in mind.

What's Motherboard Stuff Have to Do with Graphics?

On a computer equipped with a local bus motherboard, a video subsystem comes "wired" right on the motherboard. It takes the place of the video card you might buy and stick in one of the PC's expansion slots. An ordinary video card's speed is tied to that of the ordinary motherboard's expansion bus, which doesn't exceed 10 Mhz on the fastest (MCA) motherboards. Local bus video, because it's part of the CPU's immediate (or *local*) bus, can shoot instructions to the CPU and memory at nearly the CPU's operating speed—from 16Mhz to 66Mhz—in full, 32-bit-wide data streams, and with a lightning data transfer rate of 133MB/second (compared to EISA's 33MB/sec. in ultra-fast *burst mode*).

Here to Stay?

It's not quite that simple, of course. (You're rolling your eyes again.) Right now, local bus video is *proprietary*, meaning there aren't any accepted standards. Buy a PC with local bus video hardwired onto it, and you may be stuck.

> *If you use video-intensive software, local bus will give you faster performance on the video operations that don't require processing power. On the other hand, a coprocessed graphics card speeds video processing.*
>
> **BOTTOM LINE**

Local Bus Expansion Cards

And then there's the expansion card side to local bus video. You see, one of the leading local bus motherboard standards, *VL-Bus*, is basically an ISA motherboard with up to three local bus expansion slots. Currently, several video card manufacturers are eyeing the VL-Bus standard, planning to make VL-Bus versions of their graphics cards.

But you thought I said the video was already wired onto the motherboard, canceling the need for an expansion card? True, but the video card people are betting that their products offer desirable enhancements and upgradability beyond the reach of motherboard video. Once inside the VL slot, these special, VL-compatible video cards will override the motherboard's video chip. Like the video chip, the local-bus compatible cards will be able to blaze at near-CPU speeds.

Look for other VL-Bus boards, like hard disk controllers, network adapters, full-motion video, and audio boards, to emerge in the coming year.

Monitors

All this talk about blazing video cards and we've almost forgotten about *monitors*, the other, equally crucial half of the PC display equation.

Monitors come with monochrome or color capability. Most bundled with today's PCs are of the VGA or Super VGA (SVGA) variety. When driven with the corresponding video card, they can enable your PC to work with a spectrum of colors at a crisp focus. (A special black-and-white VGA monitor meant for desktop publishers shows an equally crisp image, but in a single "color.")

Keep the following considerations in mind when upgrading your monitor to VGA or SVGA.

- *Resolution:* A good monitor should be able to show resolutions matching those enabled by your video card (check out Table 9.2). Don't settle for less than 800 by 600 pixels. *Dot pitch* and *scan* (or refresh) *rates* also affect resolution. (Don't worry. They're next on the list.)

- *Dot pitch:* Buy a monitor with the *lowest* dot pitch you can afford. Measured in millimeters (mm), it's the distance between the centers of tiny points of light on your monitor. The closer the dots, the tighter the picture's focus. Optimum dot pitch is .28mm or less.

- *Refresh rate:* A flickering, muddy picture is the result of a low vertical scanning rate, or refresh rate (from the electron beams that *refresh* the phosphors living in the picture tube). Look for refresh rates above 70Hz—even higher if you purchase a giant-sized monitor, whose flicker can really make you want to throw it out the window (if you could only lift it . . .).

- *Non-interlaced scanning:* Non-interlaced (NI) monitors scan the entire screen at once instead of in alternating, flicker-inducing lines like the older, interlaced models—much easier on the eyes.

Aesthetics aren't the only reason to look for a high scanning rate. Flicker can irritate your eyes and impede your productivity.

- *Screen size:* A good size for an upgraded monitor is *15 inches* (diagonal measure), although they can go up to 20 inches and more (these weigh a ton and cost even more). In general, the larger a monitor's viewing area, the more you can see on screen at once, at higher resolutions. Windows users especially need these.

- *Resolution resizing ability:* A monitor advertised as *multiscan* or *multifrequency* should be able to adjust its video frequency automatically when it encounters alternate video modes (for example: going from the VGA mode in which you normally operate into an older program with an EGA display).

- *Comfort:* Make sure all controls are visible and within comfortable reach. You'll want controls for image brightness and contrast, as well as for sizing and positioning the image on the screen. Some

advanced monitors offer controls for adjusting colors. To mini-
mize glare while computing, buy a flat-screen model, shown in
Figure 9.1. The monitor should tilt and swivel to suit your viewing angle.

Figure 9.1

*Flat screens reduce glare
that can cause eyestrain.*

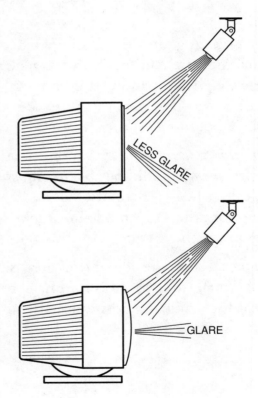

A Three-Way Deal

There's a third player on the video card/monitor team: your *software*.
Unless you have the right software drivers—and the software to give
them a purpose—your fancy video card and monitor will just sit there,
as shown in Figure 9.2. As in all computer upgrades, *find out what your
software needs* and then buy the appropriate hardware. (Wise shoppers
who don't want to repeat the upgrading ordeal for some years down
the road should buy the best monitor/video card combo they can
afford—software's always improving.)

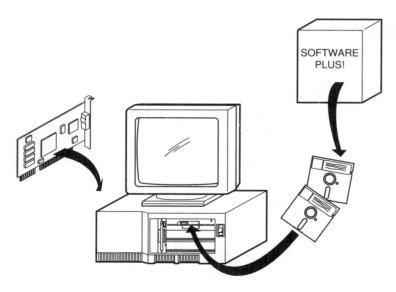

Figure 9.2

*The resolution you can
achieve on your monitor
depends on the capabilities
of the monitor, the video
card, and your software.*

Once you upgrade your PC's display, you'd do well to reconfigure the programs you use so they'll display in equally enhanced modes. With some software, you'll need to rerun its setup program.

Scanners

While we're talking about images on the screen, let's discuss some devices that put images there. A scanner lets you put pictures into your PC, ready to be added to a newsletter or transformed into Windows wallpaper. Depending on your budget and the level of image sharpness, or resolution, you require, you may choose a hand-held or flatbed scanner.

Jär-gen:

More expensive scanners can also handle text, when teamed with optical character recognition (OCR) software. This software converts the scanned letter "pictures" into ASCII text you can use in your word processor.

Hand-Held Scanners

Hand-held scanners work like the bar-code readers at the grocery store. You hold down the scanner (Figure 9.3) and guide it over the image to be scanned.

Wider scanners can work with wider images. Most can scan either a half-page (4 inches) or a full-page width (8 inches). Special software lets you "stitch" the strips together to form a complete picture.

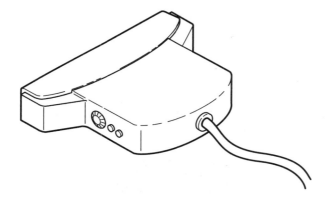

Figure 9.3

Hand-held scanners transform pictures into information your PC can process.

Hand-held scanners vary in their image quality, measured in a type of resolution termed *dots per inch* (*dpi*). As with monitors, you pay a price for sharper output, expressed in higher dpi values. Hand-helds range in price from $150 to several hundred dollars and are best suited to users with occasional scanning jobs and low budgets.

Flatbed Scanners

If a hand-held scanner works like a bar-code reader, the flatbed model works more like a copy machine. Your photo or party flier is "copied" into your PC, ready to be manipulated with software. Flatbeds are faster (you can cover more image area with a copy machine than a bar-code reader, for instance). Whether color or high-resolution gray-scale, flatbed prices have leveled out dramatically, to about $1,500 by mail-order.

Take the following guidelines into consideration when shopping for a scanner.

- *Resolution:* Look for a minimum of 300 by 300 dpi for graphics work and for reading-in text.

- *Scanbed size:* Make sure it's big enough for your typical documents and images.

- *Speed:* With scanners, speed's not everything—you may find a model that takes an extra moment, but produces a better-quality scan.

- *OCR software:* This is generally sold by third-party software companies, but make sure a package is available for the model you buy, if you intend to scan text.

- *Graphics software:* A smart suite of graphics software bundled with the scanner can increase its capabilities.

- *Cables and interface cards:* Scanners connect to your PC via a serial, parallel, or SCSI port. If it works with a SCSI interface, this should come with the scanner package; in any case, you'll need a cable.

Still Video Computer Imaging Units (Whew!)

Imagine being able to incorporate photos into your documents without using a scanner. A *still video unit* acts similarly to a camera. You take a snapshot, and the "camera" records the image as a single frame of video, onto disk instead of onto film. Some models let you dump the image right into your PC through a special expansion card; others work with tiny 2-inch diskettes that fit into miniature drives. Still others let you view the image on a TV screen with a special hookup.

These handy units have been on the market for a few years now, so look for improved technology and lower prices (well under $1,000). This is a great application for real-estate agents, model agencies, or anyone else who needs to incorporate "real-time" images into their PC programs.

In This Chapter, You Learned . . .

Upgrading a PC's display is one of the few times you'll need to shop for two complementary peripherals: a monitor and a video card. Shop carefully, and be sure to match their capabilities to that of your software. Scanners, still video units, and many other advanced graphics boards can give you new and exciting ways to take advantage of your new, enhanced PC display.

Chapter 9 Checklist: Looking at Video

For Monitors:

Brand	Model #	Price	Size	Maximum Resolution	Dot Pitch	Scanning Frequencies	Refresh Rate	Non-interlaced?
____	____	____	____	_____	____	_____	____	_____
____	____	____	____	_____	____	_____	____	_____

- Does the monitor flicker obviously when I glance at a point along its side?

- Does a multisync model switch to different resolutions automatically (autoswitch)?

- Does any glare-proofing impede visibility?

- Does it come with all cables and connectors?

- Does the salesperson recommend any special brand of video card?

- Are controls handy? Does it tilt and swivel? Will it be big enough to run multiple windows in high resolution?

For Video Cards:

Brand	Model #	Price	Resolution Modes	Pixels	Colors	Total Palette	Memory	Bit-Width
____	____	____	_____	____	____	_____	____	____
____	____	____	_____	____	____	_____	____	____

- How many resolution modes can the card produce? At what colors?

- Will the card support the monitor I like?

- If my monitor supports it, can the card adapt to older video modes like EGA or monochrome graphics?

- How much memory is included? How much more can I add later?

- Are the card's vertical scanning rate and non-interlacing (or interlacing) compatible with the monitor I like?

- How many colors will the card display? Does my application require more?

- Would my application run better with a graphics accelerator card? A coprocessed video board?

Notes: _____

_____

_____

_____

_____

_____

_____

Mastering the Art of Hard Copy

Practically everyone who buys a PC today buys a printer. It wasn't always that way. In ye computing days of olde (10 years ago), personal printers were expensive, bulky, and temperamental. Today, quality printers are affordable, and all of them ape one or more printer standards so they can work with your software.

There's a universal truth to printers: We always underestimate our printer needs. For example, most of us leave the computer store with our first PC tucked under one arm and the most basic printer model—strictly *draft-mode*—tucked under the other. We opt for the low-cost route and end up stuck with a printer that transforms our creative zeniths into 9-pin nadirs.

If there's a universal truth to PCs, it's that software grows ever more powerful and amazing. That's great. But to see the same great results on paper as you get on your computer's screen, you'll need to have a quality printer.

First, a Printer Refresher Course

If you have a copy of *The Most PC for Your Money*, this book's sibling, turn to the printer chapter for the Most Exhaustive Printer Primer. Otherwise, here's a printer jargon refresher course.

Seven Terms to Measure Printer Power

- *Dots per inch (dpi)*: The higher the number, the better a printer's output looks.

- *Near-letter quality (NLQ), draft mode,* and *letter-quality (LQ)*: These are standard printer modes.

- *Characters per second (cps)*: The higher the number, the faster a printer works.

- *Pages per minute (ppm)*: The higher the number, the faster a printer works.

- *Compatibility, Epson, IBM, HP LaserJet*: One of these brands, or able to mimic their standards.

- *PostScript,* or *PostScript emulation*: Having the PostScript printing standard or the ability to mimic it.

- *Fonts*: The more a printer offers, the more variety of type styles you get. Fonts can be *fixed* (printing well at one size) or *scalable* (able to print at any point size you decree).

Upgrade Your Existing Printer

You say your printer was state-of-the-art just a year ago? Not to worry. Somewhere there's a hardware trick to help extend your trusty printer's usefulness a year or two longer.

- *Accelerator boards*: Boost your printer's resolution by adding a new controller board. Costly ($1,500 and up) and difficult to install, this drastic upgrade's meant for people who demand the highest quality output.

- *Font cartridges*: Expand your type style selection merely by purchasing font cartridges and sliding them into the font cartridge slots found on most inkjet and laser printers (see Figure 10.1). This is one way to achieve PostScript scalable fonts on a non-PostScript printer. Cartridges cost more than downloadable software fonts (they average $400), but they don't burden your PC's RAM or hard disk space.

- *Printer buffer*: This boxy unit lets you work on other tasks while printing, by intercepting the data being sent from your PC to your printer. The printer buffer stores characters until the printer is ready for them, then feeds the characters to the printer. Buffers are primitive and hard to control, but if you can't afford extra PC RAM for a print spooler, try a buffer.

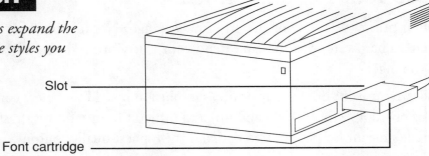

Figure 10.1

Font cartridges expand the number of type styles you can use.

Slot

Font cartridge

- *Printer RAM board*: Improve graphics performance by sliding a RAM board into your printer. Adding 4MB should cost about $200 and will jump-start your printer's graphics capabilities, including font handling and page setup speed. Printer RAM comes in many different forms, depending on the printer; an assortment is shown in Figure 10.2.

- *RAM print spooler*: This solution makes your PC *seem* faster, because you can *multitask*—that is, work with something else while your PC's printing. Speed up printing by using extra RAM from your PC as a print spooler. You can obtain software that serves as both a print spooler and a print job manager. There's more about software solutions in Chapter 3.

Figure 10.2

The type of RAM you need to add depends on your printer's manufacturer and model.

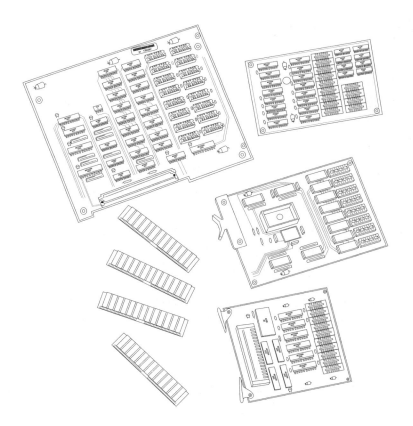

Printers for Every Situation

You're bound to meet the limits of your existing printer, eventually. Maybe you'll need to print documents during a business trip or generate color hand-outs for a big presentation. It may be time to spring for a specialty printer.

Output from the Outback

A new crop of portable printers let you output letters and reports—even the Great American Novel—wherever kismet takes you. Portable printers may not perform as quickly or easily as desktop models, but they're an essential compo-nent of any truly mobile office. And, because not everyone who buys a laptop buys a portable printer, manufacturers are loading them with extra features, hoping to sell them as double-duty desktop models.

What type of output do you require? Does your software pose any limita-tions? How long is your average stay on the road? Will the portable serve as your printer at home, too? Consider these factors first, and then look at the following features.

- *Size and weight*: If you spend more time on the road than in the hotel room, spend more time thinking about size and weight. The smallest models hardly budge the scale at 2 pounds or less. When shopping, remember to "try on" the printer in your briefcase or tote. (Before you scandalize the salesclerk, make sure to let him or her know what you are doing, first.)

- *Paper handling*: The less a printer weighs, the less capably it handles paper feeding chores. If you want a combination desktop printer/road warrior, put paper handling features before size and weight. Will it need to handle continuous-feed paper? Only a few portables do. Figure 10.3 shows a typical setup.

- *Speed*: If speedy output is important, look to the heavier models. For comparison, the fastest portables are on a par with the slowest dot-matrix desktop models, about 48 cps in quality mode.

- *Power*: Most models can run from a battery, although studies report that few people actually use the batteries they buy (and lug around). A battery boosts a portable's price by about $75; make sure you really need one. Ask how fast you can print and how many pages you'll get from one battery charge.

- *Print quality*: Most portables spit out acceptable hardcopy using inkjet technology. Per-page cost is low, about 10 cents, but the ink may look smeared or blurry. Look to thermals, the other type of portable printers, for the finest output. You'll pay more: up to 50 cents per outstanding page.

- *Standards*: Portables commonly support the Epson and IBM printer emulation standards. Some offer HP DeskJet emulation. Also, Windows users should ask if a Windows printer driver is available to squeeze full power out of their software.

Figure 10.3

Paper handling counts on a portable printer.

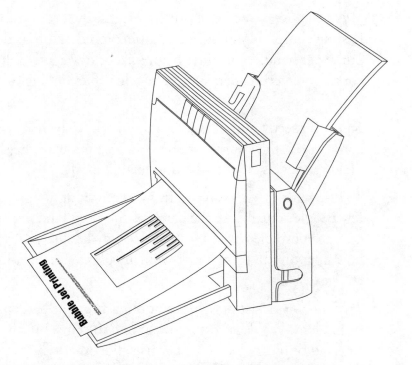

- *Cost*: Portable printers run from $300 to $500. Prices vary, so be sure to shop around. Don't forget to figure in warranty, support, and service.

Color Printers

Most PCs come with a color monitor. And many popular programs work best in color. Still, no matter how splashy the program looks on your monitor, print it out, and it fades to gray faster than Dorothy's homecoming from Oz. Dullsville! If you'd like to transfer the vibrancy of a color display to your hardcopy, there's a color printer upgrade for you.

Inkjet Color Printers

Inkjet printers work quietly, but these mid-priced color printers rarely offer PostScript emulation. They beat the cheaper dot-matrix printers in quality, but the jaggies they spit out prove they're relatively low-resolution. Color printers can't hold all possible colors, so they combine four ink colors: cyan, yellow, magenta, and black. Look for a printer with separate ink cartridges for each shade, to avoid having to chuck the composite cartridge after a single color is used up.

Solid Ink Color Printers

Its ink comes on a solid "stick" that's melted, squirted, then quickly dried, so this printer produces cleaner copies

Stash a selection of stationery—your envelopes, letterhead, forms, and mailing labels—in your car. Next time you're near the computer store, test any printers that look interesting. Simply create a few small print jobs in the software you use most often, and save these files to a handy floppy. You can hand the disk to the salesman and ask him to test a number of printers. That way, you can judge their real-world performance.

BOTTOM LINE

137

using normal paper. Solid ink printers approach laser printers in resolution quality (300 dpi), but cost a stratospheric $4,500–$9,000. If you opt for one of these, be sure to ask about PostScript emulation.

Dot-Matrix Color Printers

Noisy, blotchy, slow, and cheap—color dot-matrix printers are best left for the occasional prismatic festoon. Did I mention they're cheap? They'll add dash to your documents for $300 to $900.

Thermal Color Printers

Thermal models offer higher print quality than the other color models. They often include PostScript emulation and the ability to match Pantone colors (a color printing standard). You'll pay dearly: from $6,000 to $10,000, and you'll need to buy special, pricier paper.

Laser Printers

Maybe it's just me, but the day I brought home a PostScript laser printer, I knew I'd truly upgraded my PC's abilities (real fonts, at last). (And thanks to the Windows TrueType font standard, plenty more fonts stood ready for me to download from CompuServe with my modem.) I saw graphics that looked great on hardcopy, not just on screen. Ahh.

Laser printers work like quality copy machines and bring the same crisp lettering to your documents. Prices start in the range of an entry level PC, but if you need to perform large print jobs—or you seek quality and quiet, quick printouts—laser printers can't be beat.

- *Print quality*: Look for 300-dpi resolution (suitable for all but the fussiest tastes). Resolution is most important when printing graphics; it doesn't affect text very much, as you can see in Figure 10.4.

- *Speed*: Look for an average output speed of 6 ppm; speed decreases as your document grows more complex with fonts and graphics, and increases as you print multiple copies of a page.

- *Endurance*: Count on at least 2,500 to 5,000 pages a month, and a minimum of 300,000 pages total, with at least a five-year life span.

- *RAM*: Be sure you get at least 1MB of RAM installed on the printer, and more if you plan to print PostScript or many fonts and graphics on a page.

- *Resident fonts*: Look for a PostScript printer to come with at least 30 scalable (adjustable) fonts. Less costly, non-PostScript models should offer between 15 and 50 fonts onboard.

Figure 10.4

Text quality does not change much when you increase resolution, but graphic quality changes dramatically.

This is printed at 75 dpi.

This is printed at 150 dpi.

This is printed at 300 dpi.

- Look for a *font cartridge slot* somewhere on the printer; it may come in handy when you want to add additional typefaces, or upgrade to PostScript emulation if you buy a non-PostScript printer. The slot should accept HP-standard font cartridges, not just the printer's own (proprietary) ones.

- *Standards*: Look for HP LaserJet II compatibility, also called PCL 4, to ensure your printer will work with standard software packages. Another standard, HP LaserJet III (also known as PCL 5), offers extra font and print functions.

- *Paper handling*: A letter-sized paper tray will come with your printer. Trays in other sizes should be available. Check its ability to feed single sheets and envelopes. Test all possible print jobs before buying (envelopes spit out on my NEC Silentwriter 90 look like the *older* Elvis sat on them).

Be smart and buy an extra tray to hold letterhead or other specialty stationery. You'll save time and your prize letterhead won't look so crumpled from all the paper changing.

- *Processors*: All but the cheapest laser printers have their own, special chips inside them to control printing functions. The majority of these chips are the same type found in most PCs. Some very powerful newcomers called RISC chips are found in some of the newest laser printers. They offer more power for your print jobs, for not very much more memory. Be sure to check out at least one RISC laser printer.

- *Consumables:* Lasers use up toner, developer, and drum cartridges. Each of these can come in separate cartridges that you replace as they run out, but the best design bundles these into one unit that requires less frequent replacement (at a slightly higher cash outlay). Kyocera's Ecosys model offers a "green" alternative: its permanent amorphous silicon drum is made from the second hardest surface after diamonds, so the parts don't wear. Users just snap on a toner replacement, similar to replacing toner in a copy machine.

- *Cost:* A good, entry-level, PostScript-compatible laser printer can be bought for under $1,000, while the top-end, professional-level models climb into new-car price ranges.

Only You Can Prevent Ozone Emission

Laser printers can spew ozone into the environment—and on you, depending on how close you sit. Oooh, gross. As long as you're looking at the latest models, make sure it includes an ozone filter.

Filters run from $10 to $40. Count on replacing the filter every 50,000 copies (roughly every two years, your mileage may vary). Even with a filter, be careful to place the printer in a well-ventilated area. Look for the Underwriters Laboratories' *UL* mark to ensure the printer meets current emissions standards.

In This Chapter, You Learned . . .

Printers come in a bewildering array of sizes, shapes, and (most important to you) performance levels. You can choose to upgrade your existing printer's speed, resolution, or font stash with a number of hardware products. Or you can opt for a specialty printer: a portable, color, or laser model. This chapter presents a fairly comprehensive look at just how good the right printer can make *you* look.

Chapter 10 Checklist: Finding a Quality Printer

- Will it print at the resolution I require?

- Can I expand its RAM, its Fonts, or enable PostScript emulation later?

- Is the printer compatible with one or more leading printer standards, so I will find drivers for it in the software I buy? Which ones:

- Do I need portable printing?

- Do I need color printing?

Notes: _____

_____

_____

_____

_____

_____

_____

_____

_____

_____

Advancing Your Modeming Capabilities

Andrew's eyes darted from his clock to the pile of *Widget Monthly* magazines scattered on the floor. Midnight already! How could he possibly plow through all those articles in time to finish tomorrow's competitive outlook?

Hours later, the morning sun made Andrew squint as he sauntered down the hall to the conference room. Despite his fried eyeballs, his all-nighter had paid off in a great report. Entering quietly, he spotted Deirdre, the hot-shot new sales rep, calmly seated next to the regional manager.

"These figures from *Widgets France* can provide us with a clear route to higher European sales," Deirdre began confidently. Andrew fumed. He knew she'd started just as late on her report. And how'd she get a hold of European publications, anyway?

While Andrew had flipped through stacks of industry journals, Deirdre had flipped on her high-speed modem. One quick call to

CompuServe's Business Management InfoCenter and she had her data, sorted chronologically and by key words. Best of all, text and charts were already on disk, ready for Deirdre to import them into her word processor and wow the boss.

What's a Modem?

A *modem* is a device that allows your computer to ingest information from (*download*), or send information to (*upload*), another computer over ordinary phone lines. The two computers don't have to be the same type in order to communicate, nor do they need to share the same operating system software. The only requirement is that each computer be attached to a phone line and a *Mo*dulator/*Dem*odulator, or *modem,* for short.

Modems come in two basic models. An *internal modem* fits on an expansion card that goes inside your PC. An *external modem* sits on your desk and connects to one of the PC's serial ports. Look at Figure 11.1 to see the difference. Both types plug into a phone jack and work with your PC through special *communications* software. Which one you choose depends on whether you'd rather have the modem take up an expansion slot or a serial port (although internal modems cost a bit less).

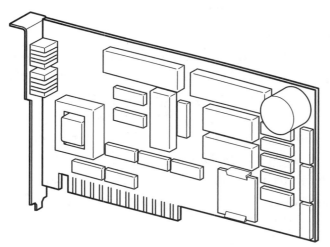

Internal modem

Figure 11.1

Typical internal and external modems.

External modem

How Does It Work?

When you're linked to the other computer, you're actually in control of that system. For example, you can type your name on your PC's keyboard, and it will show up on the screen of the PC at the other end. The modem *modulates*, or takes apart, the electronic signals from your PC and translates them into audible tones the phone system can understand. After traveling through the phone lines, the tones are *demodulated* by the modem at the other end, that is, scrambled back into electronic, digital signals that are understandable to the remote PC.

Bit Stream

Modems send data one *bit* at a time. A bit is the smallest possible unit of data a PC can handle. Bits are like tiny light switches: They're either off or on. Because computers love numbers, bits are more commonly defined as being zero (off) or one (on). That's all there is to it! A computer can only count two numbers, 0 and 1. And people think PCs are intimidating. . . .

With modems, a standard character like this *B* is made up of 10 bits—the eight bits that normally make up a text character, plus a start bit and a stop bit. A modem's communication speed is expressed in *bits per second* or *bps*. If you have a 2,400 bps modem, it sends and receives about 2,400 bits of information, or 240 characters, per second. Fast modems typically chalk up 16,800 bps.

"Huh? We Have a Bad Connection."

As you probably suspected, modems are a little more complicated than I'm letting on. For one thing, phone lines are notoriously noisy, so it's easy for errors to infiltrate your data. These blurps and bleeps are called *line noise* in modem parlance. They show up on your screen as strange characters like smiley faces and squiggles.

If you are using a modem with *error correction* or you are sending a file from one machine to another, modems handle line noise by sending little "okays?" after each information packet—sort of like nodding your head after someone tells you something, to let them know you "get" it.

A mathematical operation is performed on the information sent. The result, or *checksum*, is appended to the information packet. The receiving computer performs the same operation on the data and sees if it came up with the same result as the other PC. If the checksums don't match, the PC on the receiving end asks the sending computer to resend that information packet.

That's the technology that allows modems to get on with the business of sending and receiving, and ignore the ever-present nuisance of line noise. It's also the basis for many of today's advanced modem features like error detection/correction and data compression.

Advanced Modems

Even those readers who already have a modem won't be able to resist the modem advances coming down the pike. They're faster, smaller, and prettier. Better yet, they're smarter. Best of all, they cost almost the same as the price you paid for your fuddy-duddy modem three years ago. The following sections discuss some features you'll hear about when shopping for modems.

 **HISTORY**

Speed's the most noticeable improvement in advanced modems. Right now, we're nearing the limits of how much data can be sent over the phone line. The very latest modem standard, *V.fast*, torques up to 28,000 bps over existing phone lines. After that, we'll have to look to the all-digital phone network, *ISDN*, a primary part of our government's national high-tech agenda.

Error Correction

Error correction lets modems detect any errors caused by line noise and other greeblies. The sending modem encodes the data in a special format that allows the receiving modem to check it for errors. The receiving modem can request a resend until the sending modem gets it right.

Error correction imbues a modem with some pretty perfectionist tendencies. If the line noise is too bad, it'll just hang up. As a side effect, the methods involved in error correction increase (by about 15 percent) the speed at which modems can send information over the phone lines.

Jär-gen:

Two primary error-correction standards vie for supremacy: MNP4 (Microcom Network Protocol 4) and V.42 (a standard created by an international committee, the CCITT). V.42 is an extension of MNP4, and nearly every fast modem includes it.

NOTE

During a transmission, both modems must have the error correction feature in order for it to operate. After all, you can't speak German and expect to be understood unless the other person also speaks German.

Jär-gen:

Two major data compression standards jostle for dominance. The MNP5 (Microcom Network Protocol 5) standard is losing the popularity contest; it seems its data compression technique occasionally accomplishes the opposite effect! (Plus it can compress data only to 50 percent of its original size.) The V.42bis standard is smart enough not to expand data, and compresses way down to 25 percent.

Data Compression

Data compression is an extension of the error-correction feature found in advanced modems. As long as the modems are encoding transmitted data to detect errors, they might as well see if they can squeeze the data at the same time. (The PC and modem can process data far faster than it can be sent over the phone lines.)

The Data Squeeze

The sending modem basically looks for redundancies and repetition in the information it's sending and tries to send it as something simpler. Instead of sending "AAAAAAA," it might send the special message that eight A's are coming. The receiving modem spots this shorthand and expands the data into "AAAAAAAA" again.

The best high-speed modems include V.42bis. Once again, both modems must have the data compression feature before it can be enabled.

Portable Modems

Perhaps you need to be able to telecommunicate while you're on the road. Because they're designed for traveling light, portable modems pack a pound or less. They generally don't sport the flashy diagnostic lights or volume control of the normal external modem. Some portables offer faxing abilities. (Turn to Chapter 12 to learn more about the advantages of computer faxing.)

Generally, portable modems are battery-powered. Look for extras like carrying cases, cables, and AC power adapters. They can cost a bit more than basic models (averaging about $150), but if you don't want to lug along a big external modem, they're the best buy. Another plus: external portables can double as desktop modems. Some portable modems can be as small as a few inches in diameter, as shown in Figure 11.2.

Modem Installation

Installing a modem is easy. Read the section in Chapter 16 on expansion cards to learn how to connect an internal modem. External modems plug into your serial port, into a phone line, and into a power strip. You'll need some easy telecommunications software to get started, as well.

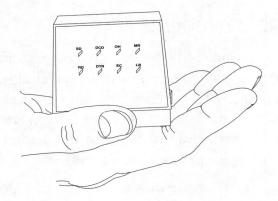

Figure 11.2

Some portable modems are extremely small, yet provide full functionality.

Standards Soup

Two modems must agree how to talk to each other (at an even more basic level than for error correction or data compression). It's as if you were trying to call someone on a radio and they were waiting by the telephone for your call; you both must agree on using either the radio or the telephone.

The most basic modem standard enables communication at 2,400 bps. If you and someone else have modems, chances are good you can connect at 2,400 bps. After that, it's a standards soup.

HST and V.32bis

The first major high-speed modem standard was U.S. Robotics' High Speed Transfer (HST) protocol. Many modems use HST. The new high-speed modem standard is *V.32bis*. This is the type of modem to buy. V.32bis modems talk to each other at 14,400 bps. (*V.32*—an older, slower standard—runs at 9,600 bps.)

Since they sport two very different standards, V.32bis modems and modems bearing the HST standard can talk together only at 2,400 bps.

Confused? The point is that it's important to select your high-speed modem carefully. Make sure you can connect to the places you want at the speed you want.

What standards are on the burner for the future? The committee that gave us V.32bis is working on the "ultimate" modem standard, *V.fast*, capable of utilizing the full possible speed of data transfer over standard phone lines, about 28,800 bps. V.fast: coming to a phone line near you.

> *One modem can talk to both V.32bis and HST modems at full speed: the U.S. Robotics Dual Standard. If you expect people with both types of modems to call and you need to provide high speed operation for both, get one of these pricey models. Otherwise, you're better off with V.32bis.*

BOTTOM LINE

In This Chapter, You Learned . . .

Advanced modems cost almost as much as slowpoke models did a few years back, but they'll save you time and cold cash in connect charges.

Data compression, error correction, and boosted speed are some of the enhancements to expect from high-end modems. Shoppers should keep a wary eye on standards, the one critical factor that keeps everything flowing smoothly.

Chapter 11 Checklist: Comparing Advanced Modems

- Would an external or internal model best suit my PC's current configuration?

- Where will I plug it in?

- Should I consider a dedicated data phone line?

- Is the modem compatible with leading standards?

- Will the modem work with other modems I need to contact at the speeds I desire?

- Should I consider a portable model?

- Do I need data compression or error correction?

- Is software offered as part of the deal?

- If I have a favorite communications software package already, will it work with the new modem?

Notes: _____

_____

_____

_____

Fax with Your Computer

Jack rustled through the papers in his file cabinet, looking for the fax he'd received from Acme Potato Supply last week. Plus, he needed the Vegetable International fax from last month. Where would that be?

"Susan, have you seen that Vegetable International fax?" he called out. "Sure have," Susan said. She pushed a few buttons, and it popped up on her screen. "Want me to print you a copy?"

While Jack depended on his trusty fax machine, Susan had opted instead for a fax card inside her computer. Now Jack, his hands full of curling thermal paper, wished he'd done the same thing.

HISTORY

Old-Time High Tech   Although "fax" just recently became a buzz word, they've been around for years. In fact, news wire services and the U.S. Weather Bureau used faxes during World War II to send and receive information. Since modems and fax machines work in such a similar fashion, they've been combined to create the latest buzz-word: a fax card.

How Does a Fax Card Work?

A *fax card* plugs into an expansion slot inside your computer; you plug
a phone cord into a jack in the back of the card. When somebody
sends you a fax, the fax card "grabs" it. Some will grab the incoming
fax in the background, letting you continue to write letters or play
computer games. Others "take over" your computer, so you have to tap
your toes for a few minutes until the fax is received.

Figure 12.1

A fax card ready for action.

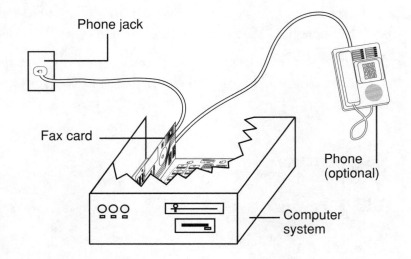

Phone jack

Fax card

Phone
(optional)

Computer
system

Once the fax is inside your computer, you can view it on the screen.
If it's important, send it to your printer. If it's a "junk fax," it can be
deleted. Faxes can be stored on your hard drive for easy reference.

Sending a fax is even easier. When you've finished your letter, push a button. The fax card will take over, converting your text into "fax format" and sending it to the fax machine of your choice.

Are They Hard to Install?

Check Chapter 16 for instructions on installing an expansion card in your PC. As long as your phone cord's nearby, installing a fax card couldn't be easier. And you don't even need an extra phone line, as long as you're willing to swap phone time for fax time.

NOTE

If you maintain only one phone line for voice, fax, and even modem communications, fine! Many people feel the extra expense isn't worth it, especially if they fax or modem infrequently. Just remember to tell others to give you a warning phone call before they fax you something, so you can set it up.

Are Fax Cards Really as Good?

Which is better, a fax card or a fax machine? Well, as with any other computer toy, the answer depends on how you'll be using it. Both come in handy at different times. In fact, it's best to have both a fax machine *and* a fax card!

Fax Cards: Pro

The next few paragraphs explain when fax cards come in handy. Keep reading after that, though, to learn why you shouldn't stick that old fax machine into the closet just yet!

Fax Cards Don't Waste Paper

Nearly every fax machine has a wastebasket sitting right next to it. Fax machines usually waste four sheets of paper for each transmission. First, a letter's printed from the computer, fed through the fax machine, and dropped immediately into the waste-basket. A second paper copy emerges from the fax machine on the other end of the phone line. That's usually photocopied and discarded in order to convert that yucky thermal paper to "normal-paper" paper. The fourth sheet of paper, the cover letter, is thrown away when the fax is received.

Fax cards don't use any paper at all. The document moves from one computer screen to another. Often, there's no need for a "real" paper document at all.

Fax Cards Can Automate Your Faxes

Since a fax card is completely computerized, it's better at automating chores. For instance, it can be programmed to send faxes to large groups of people, and at different times, in order to avoid excessive long-distance charges. The low-person-on-the-office-totem-pole won't have to stand by the machine, feeding paper through the rollers, and trying to remember who's supposed to receive what page.

Faxes Will Look Better

Faxed documents never look as good as a type-written page. That's because a fax machine "scans" them in: it takes a picture of the letter, and sends that picture over the phone lines. When it scans in the letter, it picks up creases and wrinkles, stray bits of dirt, thumb-print smudges and other foreign matter.

But a fax card skips that step; it transforms your letters and words directly into a picture. Since there's nothing mechanical involved, the copy will be a lot cleaner. Place a fax machine's fax next to one sent by a fax card. The fax card's quality will be immediately noticeable.

Fax Cards: Con

Faxes are essentially pictures: pictures of letters or newspaper articles, for instance. A fax card's software can translate your words and letters into a picture, and send it to another fax machine. But how can it translate a newspaper clipping into a picture? It can't.

That means it can't put your signature at the bottom of your letter, either. How can you sign something that's only on your computer screen? How can you send a letter on your fancy letterhead? (Hint: recreate your letterhead in your word processor, then type your fax on that; most fax cards can handle it.)

In addition, sometimes using a fax card can be a little more complicated. With a fax machine, you sign the letter, drop the paper in the bin, push the buttons, and go to lunch. With a fax card, you have to juggle your graphics on-screen, positioning everything in just the right place before sending the fax.

In fact, you'll probably want to practice sending a few faxes to a plain old fax machine to test your work until you're sure it looks right.

Fax Card Software

The software accompanying the fax card makes the biggest difference. For instance, Delrina's WinFax works directly with most major Windows word processors. You can create some fancy letterhead with Word for Windows by importing graphics files. When you're ready to print, select WinFax from your list of printers; it will appear right there on the menu.

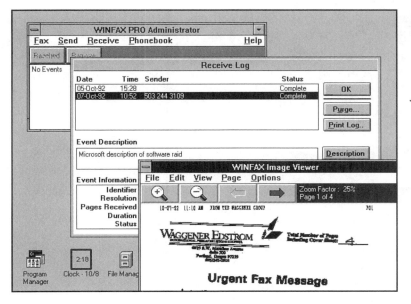

Figure 12.2

Fax software is available that lets you send faxes from within Microsoft Windows.

WinFax will convert everything into a fax, and send it buzzing through the phone lines. It's great at receiving faxes, as well. For instance, sign your name on a blank piece of paper, and fax it to your fax card using a friend's fax machine. Use Windows' paint program to "grab" that signature and save it as a graphic file on your PC. When you want to sign your faxed letters, just tell Word for Windows to import that signature graphic and stick it at the bottom of your letter!

NOTE

Faxed signatures are best reserved for your casual, day-to-day letters. The legal validity of a faxed signature is questionable, at best. (Not on your will, okay?)

In fact, Windows-based software is probably the best way to go. Faxes are graphics, and Windows' graphics-based environment makes it easier to see just what's going on.

Fax Terminology

Fax cards come with their own bundle of terms. Here's a look at the words you'll need to know before shopping for your own fax card.

- *PCX*: A file ending in these letters (say, SIG.PCX) contains graphics in a special format. You can import these graphics into most word processors and place them in your faxed letters.

- *bps*: Fax cards and machines measure the speed of their transmissions in bits per second. The higher the bps, the faster the machine.

- *fax/modem*: Since faxes and modems use pretty much the same technology, most manufacturers include a fax and modem on the same card. This can be a great money saver.

- *OCR*: Standing for Optical Character Recognition, it's a breed of software that looks at the faxed image and breaks down the picture of a document into legible words and letters. The fax, converted into text, can then be added to a word-processed document. The software's in its infancy, however. It can only recognize certain typefaces, and it's not yet 100 percent reliable.

- *scanner*: A fax machine "scans" a document, meaning it takes a picture of it and sends that snapshot over the phone lines to the other fax machine, which recreates it. Its "scanner" is built-in. Computer scanners, however, connect to your computer, letting you send the picture of your document to your computer screen for later processing. The smaller, black-and-white scanners are the cheapest, yet they might be all you need for scanning pictures,

> Most of today's fax/
> modem cards say 9600
> on the box. Check
> carefully; 9600 bps is
> standard for faxes, so
> that's nothing special.
> Most fax/modem cards
> don't include a high-
> speed modem, however,
> so check the fine print. It
> will probably say 2400
> bps somewhere, which
> will usually be the speed
> of the modem. This is
> changing quickly,
> however, as products
> improve. Soon the modem
> bundled on fax/modem
> combos will be up to a
> faster speed, as well.

BOTTOM LINE

newspaper articles, and signatures into your computer. The most expensive scanners can use color, and look like small copy machines.

- *Group III*: Make sure your fax card is Group III-compatible, so it will work with the majority of fax machines released in the past five years.

Faxing from the Road

Laptops can send faxes just as easily as desktop computers. Many laptops come with fax/modems built in; others offer them as upgradable (albeit expensive) options. But before springing for a fax/modem, make sure you'll really need one while on the road. Do you really need to send faxes? Or can you just send your data using a modem?

Also, some on-line services like CompuServe will send faxes for you. Send your letter to CompuServe using your modem, enter the fax's phone number, and CompuServe will fax it for you, even repeating the process if the fax's phone number is busy. However, you must have an account on CompuServe before you can go this route.

In This Chapter, You Learned . . .

Fax cards automate the tedious (but ubiquitous) modern-day task of sending faxes. You can buy fax/modem combinations that save expansion slots in your PC. These products vary in performance and price, and are flooding the market in ever-increasing numbers. They can save you cash, as well as expansion-slot space for more important upgrades down the road.

Chapter 12 Checklist: Faxing with Your Computer

- Does the fax card include a modem?
- What should I look for in fax software (i.e., do I need one that works under Windows)?
- Will my application require that I buy a scanner, as well?

Notes: _____

_____

_____

_____

The Multimedia Workstation

"I'll use this new Multimedia upgrade to create business presentations," Jerry told himself, as he plopped down his credit card at the Computer Superstore. "Of course, the kids can learn math and spelling with one of the educational CDs that came bundled with the package."

He came home, pushed his wholesome intentions to the back of his mind, pushed the compact disc into the front of his PC, and started pushing buttons on his joystick, scooting his Nova 9 spacecraft over the planet's craggy surface, keeping a wary eye out for Gir Draxon's lethal drones.

What's Multimedia?

A *medium* is a way of conveying information. *Multimedia* means combining media—sound and video, for instance. An ordinary television set could be called "multimedia." In fact, while the computer industry tries to label multimedia as a "serious business tool," most consumers recognize multimedia for what it is: entertainment, just like television.

But it's expensive entertainment, unfortunately. Computers were designed to store numbers and words, not rollicking sounds and splashy video. That's where the upgrade comes in: enabling your PC to handle music and pictures.

It's relatively easy for a computer to play sounds and video. Sound cards pop inside a computer, hook up to a pair of speakers or a home stereo, and play back music and sound effects. And most of today's high-quality video cards and monitors can already play back "television-like" movies.

Multimedia Checklist

Unfortunately, the MPC standard keeps changing as computers become more powerful. Basically, here's what your machine will need to qualify as an "official" multimedia PC:

- A 386 or more powerful microprocessor.

- The Microsoft Windows operating environment, plus Windows-compatible software.

- A 100MB hard drive.

- A Super VGA monitor.

- A joystick (game) port.

- A CD-ROM drive.

- A sound card that has digital sound and an onboard synthesizer.

- A pair of speakers.

- An inexpensive microphone (optional, but invaluable for embedding "Get to work" sound bites in your e-mail memos).

Know Your Ingredients

Some companies sell "Multimedia-ready" PCs, straight out of the box. Or, you can upgrade your PC to multimedia standards in two ways: buying a multimedia upgrade package, or buying all the parts separately and installing them yourself. Either way, here's what to look for in the individual components.

Sound Cards

Sound cards are expansion cards that enable your PC to blare sounds; that part's obvious. But the key is understanding the two kinds of sounds: digital and synthesized. The two types may sound similar, but they're very different.

Digital sound consists of sound waves that have been recorded on a PC. A recorded scream, for instance, or the sound of a cello quartet at the symphony hall last night, would be digital sound. The sound card records by turning sound waves into numbers; it plays digital sound by converting the numbers back into sound waves.

Synthesized sounds, on the other hand, originate from the sound card itself, a modern version of the "Moog" synthesizers of the '60s. One of the first sound cards, called AdLib, set a standard for synthesized sound that's still followed by most software today.

AdLib holds the synthesized-sound market, and a card called the SoundBlaster has the handle on the digital sound market. To run the most DOS software, make sure your sound card is compatible with both AdLib and SoundBlaster. This rule of thumb is slowly changing, however, as more multimedia applications run under Windows. As long as your card contains drivers for Windows 3.1, you're safe.

BOTTOM LINE

NOTE

Most sound cards come with a small amplifier built-in. You'll have to supply the speakers, however. For the best sound, run a cable from the "out" jack on the sound card to an "in" line on your home stereo system. Then you can really hear Gir Draxon scramble to avoid those laser blasts!

What Can I Expect to Pay for PC Sound?

Look to spend anywhere from $100 to $300 on a sound card. It all depends on the quality your application requires. (See? Software calls *all* the shots when it comes to PCs!) For professional, music-industry quality, count on spending more than $1,000. If you're interested in this level of PC sound enhancement, however, you'd be wise to visit user groups where other PC/music enthusiasts gather. (If you're investing in this level of music hardware/software, you're facing a huge cash outlay—so seek the opinions of experts on current products.)

Video Cards, Monitors, and PC TV

Most Super VGA cards installed in computers can already handle the demands for multimedia video. And most VGA or better monitors can show off all the neat new things multimedia can do. (You'll need to consult Chapter 9 if you still need to upgrade your computer's "good looks.") However, a new computer toy has arrived: PC TV! That's right: a television on a card.

By plugging a card into one of your computer's internal slots, you can see a television screen on your monitor. Some cards fill the monitor with a TV picture; others reduce the TV picture to a small window. When placed in the corner of the screen, the "TV window" lets you watch the stock market reports, for example, while updating a spreadsheet. (Or watch soap operas while at work!)

Images from the screen can be captured to disk for later use. A Candice Bergen close-up from a "Murphy Brown" episode can turn up as Windows wallpaper; add a sound card, and you can hear a perpetually obnoxious laugh track as well!

The main drawback to these "TV cards" comes with their price tag. Shooting skywards at more than $500, they're several times more expensive then a real (desktop) TV. It all comes down to what your application requires; if you need to screen full-motion video, this is the upgrade you'll need. Other, more advanced expansion boards increase your PC's ability to alter and output video images.

CD-ROM Multimedia Quarterback

One problem comes with storing all those sounds and pictures; they take an enormous amount of space. A floppy disk can barely hold ten seconds of speech. So, a new component has entered the scene: the *CD-ROM drive*.

CD-ROM drives work much like the compact disc players in your home stereo. Just like the CD drive in your stereo, these CDs can only be played. You can't write information to them with your computer. You pop in a CD, and your computer can grab the sounds and pictures from it. CDs can hold much more information than an average hard disk (and way more than any floppy)—making these laser-etched frisbees a natural for multimedia fun.

ISTORY

To software aficionados, "compact disc" may look like a misspelling. The "c" in "disc" is a holdover from the CD's origins in the music industry; *disc* meant "record" long before there were floppy *disks* for PCs.

Internal and External Drives

CD-ROM drives come in two flavors, internal and external (see Figure 13.1). The internal ones fit into the front of your computer, just like a floppy disk. When you push a button, a tray pops out. Drop the compact disc into the tray, push the tray back in, and you're on your way. External CD-ROM players come in a separate box that sits next to your PC; a cable connects to your PC's back end. Both varieties work with your PC by means of an expansion card that sits in one of your PC's slots.

Audio-Files for Audiophiles!

Most CD-ROM drives come with an *audio port*, usually called an *earphone jack*. That means you can listen to your favorite compact discs while you work! Unfortunately, you can't listen to an audio CD and access your CD-ROM drive at the same time. In fact, that's why you need a sound card in addition to a CD-ROM drive. The compact disc merely drops information into your computer. The sound card and video card then handle the chores of converting that information into sounds or pictures.

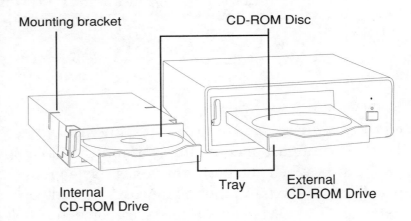

Compact disc (CD-ROM) drives come as internal or external units.

Mounting bracket

CD-ROM Disc

CD-ROM Disc

Internal
CD-ROM Drive

Tray

External
CD-ROM Drive

HISTORY

MPC   When multimedia hit the market a few years ago, a group of manufacturers were ready. They'd already learned something from the VHS/Beta VCR wars a decade earlier. They decided to create a standard for multimedia early on. They dubbed the new standard *MPC*, a wildly creative acronym meaning Multimedia PC.

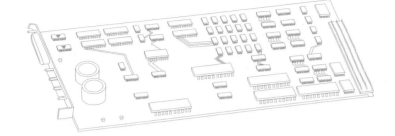

Figure 13.2

A sound card fits into your PC's expansion bus.

What Does CD-ROM Cost?

Depending on their features, CD-ROM drives currently cost from about $300 to more than $1,000. Depending on your application, you can get away with a slower, cheaper drive for less, especially if you need to access mostly no-frills, text-based data from one of the many databases that come on CD-ROM discs. If you need to play killer sound and animations, though, prepare to dig deep in your pockets. (Yeah, I know—all the fun stuff always seems to keep the ol' credit card balance off kilter.)

Multimedia Upgrade Kits

Some companies sell kits designed to upgrade your PC automatically for multimedia fun. CompuAdd and Media Vision both sell a bundled kit containing a sound card and CD-ROM drive. When buying a

How slow can you afford to go? When buying CD-ROM drives, look for its data-transfer rate and its average track-seek time. The first number describes how quickly your CD-ROM drive can move information from the compact disc into your computer; the second number describes how quickly the drive can find the right information on the disc. For best performance, look for a data-transfer rate of at least 150 kilobytes per second, and an average track-seek time of one second or less.

BOTTOM LINE

bundled upgrade kit, you'll not only get a "matched set" of equipment that works well together, but you'll get some extras: compact discs containing games and reference works, and software letting you connect the sound card to a synthesizer/keyboard, to write songs or play back special Musical Instrument Digital Interface (MIDI) music files.

The disadvantages of buying a bundle? Well, you don't get to choose your own sound card and CD-ROM drive, meaning you usually won't get the most state-of-the-art package.

Media Vision sells a complete multimedia kit containing everything: a CD-ROM drive, a sound card, and speakers bundled into a separate case that resembles a boom box. By setting the case near your computer, you can upgrade without the inconvenience of taking apart your computer and dropping in individual components.

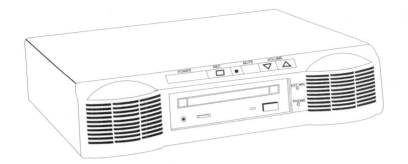

Figure 13.3

The Media Vision multimedia kit offers an all-in-one solution.

NOTE

When buying CD-ROM drives or sound cards, make sure it's easy to change their volume. The volume knob is on the back of some sound cards, hindering your attempts to turn down the sound when a game's sound track belts out a hideous scream. Some CD-ROM drives have a volume knob on the front. Look for a sound card where the volume is controlled by the software; that way you can just punch a button on your keyboard to turn the sound up or down.

Roamin' and a-ROMmin'!

Need to take your sound on the road? Then look for Media Vision's AudioPort. About the size of a pack of cigarettes, it plugs into your laptop's printer port. A small built-in speaker then plays back the sound and music data stored on the laptop's hard disk. The sound won't be as loud or flashy as an Ozzy Osbourne concert, but it's loud enough for small boardroom presentations. (Or for boring airplane flights, until the flight attendant asks you to turn it down!)

In This Chapter, You Learned . . .

Readying your PC for the multimedia boom that's been "just around the corner" for years now is possible, but it requires several upgrades. You'll need a sound card, a CD-ROM drive, and a SVGA card; you'll want at least a VGA monitor, as well. What you'll pay depends on what you'll use the setup for. If you just plan to access a few encyclopedia entries from the CD-ROM drive or add voice bites to your spreadsheets, you'll pay less for these components than if you were creating artsy, cutting-edge PC presentations.

Chapter 13 Checklist: Mulling Over Multimedia

- What software, if any, do I own now that works with multimedia hardware?

- What hardware requirements does this software have? Future software I'm interested in running?

- What CD-ROM software titles look like ones I'd like to run?

- Do these packages work with all brands of CD-ROM drives? Any incompatible models to watch out for?

- Does my PC have room for an internal drive?

- Does my sound card come with an amp built-in? Where's the volume knob?

- Does my application require one of the advanced video editing expansion boards?

Notes: _____

_____

_____

_____

_____

Taking It on the Road

By now, you're The PC Upgrade-Meister. But wait. There's something else. One last, ultimate computer upgrade, to satisfy the Wanderlust that lies deep within us all: Going Mobile.

A laptop is a completely different animal, and just about everything about it works differently. Keep that in mind while shopping, and you'll end up with a system that can really move!

Decide What You'll Use It For

Whatever size of portable you settle on, be sure to decide beforehand what you intend to do with it. After that, your decision will fall into place quicker than dust on a monitor.

Portable computers use different parts, and offer a new lexicon of jargon and terms to decipher. Other than that, the process of buying a laptop isn't all that different from buying a desktop model.

Jär-gen:

Laptops aren't even called laptops anymore! The smallest ones measure little more than a Big Mac; they're called organizers. Some of the slightly larger palmtops run DOS-compatible software; just don't trip over the teeny keyboard. Then there's sub-notebooks, bigger than palmtops, but smaller and lighter than their notebook ancestors. When a laptop's not really fit for a lap, it's called a luggable.

1. Decide what tasks you'll want your portable to perform.

2. Track down the software that performs the job.

3. Check out that software's minimum requirements.

4. Find the lightest portable with the most suitable screen and keyboard that can handle that software.

5. Buy the portable that meets your needs from the dealer who offers the best price, warranty, and service plan.

Fill Your Needs (Not Your Luggage)

Take a sheet of paper and jot down all the tasks you want your mobile unit to perform. Word processing? On-the-road faxes? Spreadsheets and other math-oriented work? Graphics? All of these tasks make different demands on a portable computer. Take an extra moment with your task list. The tasks you deem most important will carry a lot of weight (especially when your new computer is dangling from your shoulder at the airport).

For instance, do you need a floppy drive? They're indispensable on a desktop model, but unless you work with numerous files between several computers, dispense with it for your portable. When you need to move your road-gathered information to a desktop computer, you can connect the two machines with a serial cable and null-modem adapter, and zip the files back and forth. It's admittedly a little awkward, but so's a heavy laptop. And a floppy drive definitely adds weight.

How often do you work with numbers? If spreadsheets or other number-heavy applications feature prominently on your career path, figure that in when testing the portable's keyboard. On some models, the number keys are buried under other keys—accessible only after a session of finger "Twister."

Function Drains Power (Yours and the Battery's)

If you won't be using a feature very often, don't buy it. The key here is weight. Six pounds may not seem like much at the computer store, but try this: Rest the computer on your shoulder for two minutes. Now, imagine how your shoulder-bone zone will feel after two hours of the same pressure, especially when a shoulder strap has been digging into your tender flesh.

Every feature you add on to a laptop not only adds weight, but increases the drain on its batteries, as well. Now you're beginning to understand the way to buy the perfect laptop: Keeping it small and light not only makes it easier to carry around, but easier for your batteries to hold out during those transcontinental Solitaire sessions!

What Model's Best for Me?

Palmtop to luggable—and every model in-between—each has its pluses and minuses, depending on the most important factors: you and your needs.

Where'd I Put That Address? Get an Organizer!

If phone numbers and to-do lists threaten to bury you in sticky notes, perhaps you don't need a laptop at all. The pocket calculators of the '70s have turned into the pocket computers of the '90s. Today's pocket-sized "organizers" can perform dozens of computing features (see Figure 14.1). Sharp's "Wizard" series of personal organizers will not only keep track of your appointments and phone numbers, but can connect to modems to check your "electronic mail" while on the road. They can even use special software "cards" to do everything from designing draperies to managing stock portfolios.

What *can't* these "organizers" do? They can't handle large files. And the keyboards and displays are too small for serious word processing. But for tracking travel expenses and keeping a long battery life, they can't be beat for convenience.

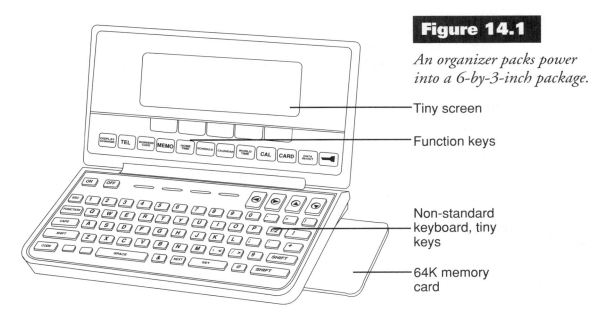

Figure 14.1

An organizer packs power into a 6-by-3-inch package.

Tiny screen

Function keys

Non-standard keyboard, tiny keys

64K memory card

Palm Power

A DOS user to the death? You may be satisfied with a palmtop computer, like Atari's Portfolio, or Hewlett-Packard's HP95 series. Memory management's the key here: RAM not only provides program working space but serves as a "hard disk" as well, thanks to the "saving" grace of a small internal battery.

Optional credit-card sized software modules slip in and out of these palmtops, expanding on their preinstalled database, spreadsheet, and word-processor modules. You can add an optional external card reader unit to your desktop's expansion bus for seamless data transfer between computers (see Figure 14.2). Another optional card expands the Portfolio's 128K storage/memory capacity to 4MB.

If you need to run large-scale programs, however, or require a full-scale (touch-type-able) keyboard or display, count on dishing out another thousand for a "real" notebook computer.

Figure 14.2

*Palmtops provide DOS
compatibility for under
1 lb.*

Sub-Notebooks

Bigger than a palmtop, sporting more memory—and even the occasional hard drive—are the sub-notebook models, relative newcomers to the portable scene. Count on better keyboards and displays on these lightweight (under 3 pounds) computers; they're still not quite on a par with notebook or desktop models, however.

I Need a Notebook

Power user? Take a look at these. Measuring up to a typical school notebook in size, these portables can be tossed into a briefcase (see Figure 14.3). Barely tipping the scale at 7 pounds, most come with a VGA screen, 386-class (or better) processor, generous hard drive, 3 1/2-inch floppy drive, and full-sized keyboard. Figure 14.4 shows how notebooks and subnotebooks compare.

Couldn't One Computer Suit All My Needs?

One of the many drawbacks to portables (dismal displays, cursable cursor keys) is the hassle of transferring files between your desktop and mobile computer. One strategy on the horizon just may solve all these problems at once: the desktop expansion station, or *docking station*.

Your notebook's fine for road use, but once you get home, you'd rather be on your full-sized monitor at your full-sized keyboard. With a docking station, simply slide the notebook into an expansion base, press firmly, and you have access to the regular amenities—as well as ports, power supplies, and a large, fast, desktop-level hard drive. Pop the levers and grab the notebook when it's time to hit the road.

Figure 14.3

Notebook computers fit neatly into a briefcase.

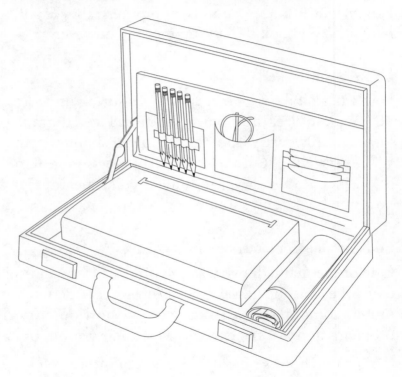

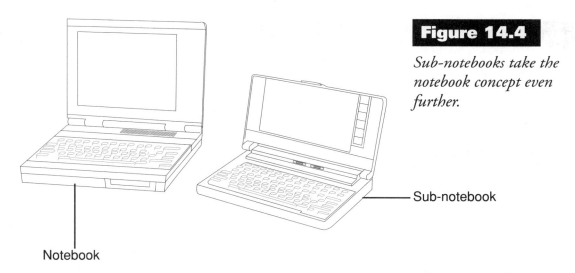

Figure 14.4

Sub-notebooks take the notebook concept even further.

Sub-notebook

Notebook

You'll pay a price for this versatility. Since they're new, expect to pay in the $5,000–$6,000 range for the notebook-and-base unit. Tack on some more for the external monitor and keyboard that make life easier. As more manufacturers catch on to the expansion station concept, expect prices to drop. This just may be the one-computer answer . . . the ultimate upgrade.

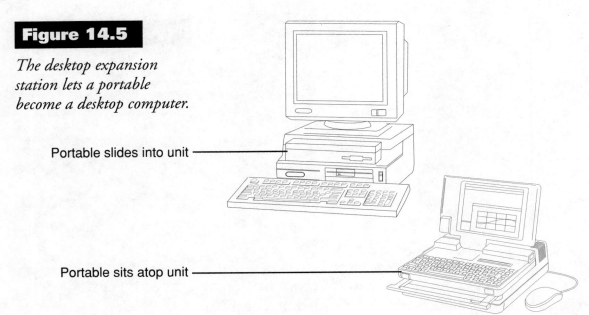

Figure 14.5

*The desktop expansion
station lets a portable
become a desktop computer.*

Portable slides into unit —————

Portable sits atop unit —————

Look Carefully at These, No Matter
What Model You Buy

Some features must be scrutinized very closely on portables. These
include keyboards, displays, disk drives, battery/power management,
and RAM/ROM cards.

Keyboards

A portable computer's keyboard may look the same as the one on your desktop, but look closely. The same keys will probably be there, but in different locations. Look for the word *full travel,* meaning the keys can be depressed just as far as on your desktop computer's comfortable keyboard.

You may find a *trackball* lurking among the keys. You move the ball with your thumb and the pointer scuttles across the screen. This portable version of mousing is fun, and essential for applications like desktop publishing or spreadsheets.

Look for the cursor keys to be arranged in an "inverted T." This makes it easy to tell which key does what, even if you aren't looking at the keyboard. Avoid special function keys, too (for example, some layouts have you hold down a special key and press the Up cursor key to mimic the "PgUp" key found on regular keyboards).

Displays

Laptop displays are based on *liquid crystal display* technology, similar to digital watches. These screens often improve upon desktop CRTs in matters like screen flicker or distortion. Look for screens with Supertwist, where ultra-flexible molecules catch the light better. Make sure the screen tilts easily and offers a range of viewing angles. Although the newer active-matrix screens offer crisper displays and better color, they won't be "cheap" for some time.

Color Portables

You can expect great things from today's color portables. For one, expect to pay a high price for a color portable, thanks to the trade restrictions on the superior thin-film transistor (TFT) active-matrix displays. (Passive-matrix displays cost less, but don't offer the bright, rich hues or stunning contrast of the active-matrix models.) On the bright side, pricing is always driven by supply and demand, so count on TFT display prices to fall as computer store shelves fill with these models.

Color impacts a unit's weight, video performance, battery life, and display quality, so watch how quickly the screen redraws, and how long it'll keep up. *Before* you buy, ask yourself if you honestly like the way it looks (you'll be looking at it a long time). Ask questions about power management and hard disk speed/capacity, in addition to CPU power, memory, and other performance concerns. Finally, sit down and see how it feels.

Floppy Drives and Hard Drives

You'll want a hard drive, preferably one equipped with the latest energy-saving features. Think twice about springing for a floppy drive. They add weight, cost more, and drain precious battery resources. If the portable will be your sole computer, however, you should add a floppy drive so you can load software into the PC.

Batteries

As laptops grow more feature-laden, battery life diminishes. Look for power-saving features like Intel's SL line of chips, designed to save power by cutting off juice to parts not being used. "Auto Resume" mode lets you turn your portable off, and when you turn it back on, you find yourself right where you left off in your software. Ask whether the battery recharges, and how long it takes. Also, be sure you get an AC adapter for use in hotel rooms or at home, to save on your batteries. Ask if surge protection's available for the adapter, as well.

RAM/ROM Cards

Mentioned in the section on palmtops, these credit-card software "disks" can be read from and (in the case of RAM cards) written to: a tiny battery keeps track of your data. No moving parts are involved, meaning less wear and tear and longer battery life.

In This Chapter You Learned . . .

A portable computer expands your horizons so intensely, it just may be the ultimate upgrade. Although the procedure for buying a portable is the same as for buying a PC, the actual components differ in many ways from their desktop brethren. Be extra selective when putting together the best portable for your money, since you'll "wear" every feature.

Chapter 14 Checklist: Trying on a Laptop

- Under what conditions will I use my laptop?

- Do I need to look at more lightweight models, or should I shop more for other (heavier) features?

- Is it too heavy to carry? Will I ever have to wear it for hours (at a tradeshow, on a walking tour, etc.)?

- Do I like the display? Are the keys comfortable?

- Does it come with software transfer software? Cables? Batteries? Do I need to buy a separate AC/adapter? Will I need to consider surge protection?

- Is it powerful enough (or too powerful, i.e., heavy) to run my applications?

- Should I consider buying a mini-trackball to navigate graphical interfaces or spreadsheets more easily?

Notes:_____

_____

_____

_____

_____

Where to Buy Your Upgrades

Lots of people buy their PC upgrades through the mail. Yet some folks still feel shaky about mail-order computer stuff. These wary types prefer to shop in person. After all, it's one thing to return a mail-order sweater because the sleeves are too long—but a delicate hard drive? A 90-pound monitor?

Besides, even if you use magazines and catalogues to research a buy, nothing beats a visit to a computer store for that "hands-on" evaluation. But what's the best type of store to visit? Or, if you muster enough courage to pick up the phone, how do you know you can trust the mail-order company?

Perhaps you'll buy your upgrades from the same place you bought your PC. Or maybe you seek a different level of service and support this time around. Well, there are almost as many ways to buy upgrades as there are upgrades to buy. And each outlet comes with pros and cons.

Upgrading Through Computer Stores

How can you tell whether a store's reliable? First, discreetly ask the staff people you meet how long they've worked there. High turnover's a bad sign. Store managers who know how to treat their staff know how to treat their customers. Is the sales staff knowledgeable and courteous? That's a great start. If they're crabby before you even make a buy, think how it will be when you're trying to return your purchase . . .

Here are some less obvious tips to help you size up a computer store or mail-order vendor. If a dealer can answer the following questions to your satisfaction, and the prices and selection please you, buy your PC's new upgrade from him or her.

What Type of Store Is the Best?

It seems like everyone's getting into selling computers these days. Each store below differs slightly in levels of selection, support, or discounting.

- Local clone sellers generally stock the best-selling, most popular components. Expect the staffers to be highly knowledgeable. They'll help you select (and possibly even install) your upgrade, especially if they have experience.

- National retail chains with names like Businessland and ComputerLand target the corporate buyer. Prices vary on upgrade items. Selection may be limited to well-known, high-recognition brands, or high-ticket items only, like monitors. Official support should be excellent here, possibly *sans* the personal touch a local clone seller can offer.

- Computer Superstores stock a huge, ever-changing variety of components. Once you manage to flag down one of the salespeople, they're helpful, even if they seem a bit harried. Free classes are often part of the deal. Don't forget to negotiate on price, installation, or warranty (or all three!).

- Membership warehouse stores offer sizable discounts on name brands. Possible tradeoffs include limited selection on upgrade components. Some stores offer tech centers, where staffers can be highly knowledgeable. However, if a warehouse store doesn't feature a specially trained staff, don't expect the salesperson to be super-familiar with late-breaking product developments. Ask about support and service policies. If your components need repair, they may have to endure being shipped back to the manufacturer. (This is hard on you and the component.)

Mail-Order Outlets Differ, Too

A bewildering array of mail-order companies offer their own set of pros and cons. Here are some pointers on this intimidating-but-economical way to shop.

Most of the larger mail-order vendors run electronic bulletin board systems (BBSs). Here, customers who have modems can call and obtain utility programs to improve their PCs. In addition, these BBSs offer tech support, and give users a place to exchange information.

There's one drawback. Although users share electronic mail about problems and hassles with the vendor's equipment, there's a chance that the vendor may censor the more derogatory messages. (After all, it's the vendor's BBS, and complaints aren't good for business.)

*There's a way to hear more objective reports from past customers, but you'll need a temporary account, or guest account, on an on-line service like CompuServe. Just log onto the vendor's forum (or discussion area), found by typing **Find**, space, and the name of the vendor.*

Even though the vendor sponsors these discussion groups, users here freely discuss issues, swap hints and tips, and download the same programs and fixes that are available on the vendor's own BBS. Plus you won't have to make a toll-call. (America Online, Delphi and GEnie are some of the other on-line services that carry vendor forums.)

Sometimes top executives are available for "conference calls," where they discuss users' questions. And you can flame (leave crabby e-mail for) the company president if his company's not responding to other complaint channels!

General Mail-Order Marketers

They have names like PCs Compleat and USA Flex, and sell an enormous variety of PCs, monitors, hard disks—even floppy disks and software—from a huge range of manufacturers. They're found in the backs of PC magazines, where their ads take up several closely-printed pages (read the fine print first!). Some charge shipping, which you should never have to pay.

Before you buy from general mail-order marketers, try to get feedback from past customers. Attend a meeting of a user group, or a computer club at a local university. PC/ Computing magazine features a monthly "Phantom Shopper" column (the writer calls anonymously, orders stuff, and reports his findings on competence, honesty, support, and reliability). Most libraries carry PC/ Computing; you'd be smart to spend an afternoon searching back issues for write-ups on the mail-order company you're considering.

BOTTOM LINE

**ISTORY**

"For Big Blue, Press One . . . " Traditionally, the big-name PC vendors like Toshiba, IBM, and Digital Equipment have shunned the direct market (mail-order), selling through the dealer channel instead. These vendors just figured that PCs were too scary for anyone to want to buy without a dealer nearby to hold their hand. The direct PC-sellers like Dell and Northgate have forced Mr. Big's hand, however, with their astonishing success in marketing PCs directly to the public. IBM, ALR, Toshiba, DEC and other dealer-only vendors are quickly jumping on the direct-marketing channel. This is a great development for us, the buyers, since support and service levels should grow even more competitive.

Direct PC Sellers

With names like Dell and Gateway, these direct marketers sell only their own brands. These PCs and components can cost slightly more than no-name clones. Direct PC sellers compete heavily for customers by outdoing each other in service and warranty policies. Look here for affordable and speedy on-site service contracts. Toll-free support goes without saying (but ask anyway!). And these vendors sponsor in-house BBSs where users can download useful programs and documentation, chat with other users, and keep up with product news. Many of these vendors offer upgradable PCs, covered in Chapter 3.

Component-Specific Vendors

They concentrate on one thing only: memory, motherboards, hard drives, or some other specific product. Theoretically, this level of focus lets the *component-specific vendors* develop expertise in their product. Call and check this out for yourself. Because these vendors move a large volume of merchandise, their prices (and selection) should be great.

Used Components

Computer swap-meets and users' groups are good places to find used components. Brokerage firms that deal in used PCs may have items you need, as well. Try the American Computer Exchange, 800/786-0717; the Boston Computer Exchange, 800/262-6399; the Computer Exchange Northwest; 206/820-1181 or the Western Computer Exchange, 505/265-1330. As with buying any used equipment, *caveat emptor* (let the buyer beware). Try to get whatever documentation, manuals, etc. are available.

Help with Installing the Stuff You Buy

Have you ever noticed how some people can't *stand* to ask for directions? Even if they're hopelessly lost and two hours late—no sir, they just can't bring themselves to pull over into one of the zillion gas stations on every corner and ask the way. Well, if you're one of those people, you probably will laugh out loud at the next suggestion, which is: Ask the dealer if they provide installation pointers, just in case you need a hand.

Okay, I've said it, so now you can just go "hrmmpfh" and keep reading. For you (that small minority) who welcome friendly assistance when you need it, make sure your dealer will oblige. (Obviously, mail-order upgraders will have to speak slowly, go step-by-step, and be extremely precise when obtaining help over the phone!)

Threading Your Way Through Warranty and Service Lingo

In the section above on how to check out a dealer, you saw some brief items about warranty and service policies. That's important stuff, so here it is again, expanded.

First, Reputation

Attend a user-group meeting, and ask members about their mail-order experiences. Is there any recurring theme in the horror stories (a particular dealer's name, perhaps)? Call the mail-order vendors that interest you, and ask how long they've been in business. Try asking for customer references (don't be disappointed if you don't get any, though).

Service and Repair

Have the dealer send you a brochure that lists their sales and support policies in writing. Don't buy unless you get a 30-day, money-back guarantee. Many dealers charge a "restocking" fee for returned merchandise. Ask about this. If they press it, don't bother with this dealer; you should never agree to a restocking fee.

Make sure the mail-order company has on-site repair facilities. You don't want your PC enduring any more shipping than is absolutely necessary. And insist on reasonable turnaround time on repairs. The dealer should pay all repair-related shipping costs. If you decide to return the item within the 30-day guarantee period, and call the dealer to obtain authorization, the dealer also should pay shipping costs on returns. After all, they want your repeat business, and good referrals build a customer base.

Warranties

Examine the dealer's warranty policy. If they fail at all, electronic systems will do so within the first 30 days. Negotiate a one-year, parts-and-labor warranty. While you're at it, ask for a two-year, parts-and-labor warranty. (Don't be disappointed if the dealer settles on a two-year, parts *or* labor warranty, however—it's tough to get a full warranty extended to two years.)

Who will honor the warranty? If you're buying from an outlet that stocks only their own brands, that base is covered. Otherwise, make sure it's the dealer—not the manufacturer—who backs the warranty with service. It's hard enough to keep track of all your upgrades without keeping track of manufacturers' phone numbers, addresses, shipping records, and technical support on each component.

Support

Look for toll-free technical support, during expanded hours, and preferably some evenings or weekends. If English is not your best language, make sure the company has customer service representatives you can understand.

Shipping

Ask how soon they'll ship the item. Nail down a firm ship date, and don't let them debit your credit card before the merchandise ships. Ask about policy on a package lost in shipment. Most vendors ship UPS ground. Make sure you get the dealer to pay for a *ground tracking number* (75 cents extra, and worth lots more). A company doesn't have to pay for a returned item to be shipped outside of the 30-day guarantee period.

Credit Cards Count

Pay for your upgrade with a credit card, if possible. You may choose to pay off your purchase when your bill comes, yet you keep the consumer protection many cards provide. (Be sure to check with your bank card company to verify what protection you're entitled to, before you make a huge purchase.) For example, if you don't receive the item as shipped, you can request your money back from the bank within 120 days.

Some mail-order houses tack on an extra fee for credit card purchases, 3 to 7 percent. Don't pay it! Instead, report it immediately to your credit card company—you may not have to pay the surcharge. Also, verify that the vendor charges your account only after the system is actually shipped. Determine in advance how billing takes place, so there won't be any surprises.

In This Chapter, You Learned . . .

An alarming variety of dealers and mail-order companies vie for your upgrade dollar. Relax, take your time, and remember that nobody's doing you a favor by selling you a component. Ask plenty of questions about sales and support policies, and run each company through the questions in this chapter and in the checklist.

Chapter 15 Checklist

Here are some questions to ask about any vendor from which you buy system components:

- Does your local Better Business Bureau show any problems with this vendor?

- (For mail-order firms): Is the vendor approved by the NYC-based Direct Marketing Association (212/768-7277)?

- Does the vendor offer on-site repair facilities?

- Does the vendor or dealer handle repairs, instead of shipping to the manufacturer?

- How long has the company been in business?

- Is the store neat, well-stocked?

- (For mail-order firms): Does the vendor specialize in a specific component area (or have knowledgeable staff)?

- Does the dealer stock a variety of components in all price/performance levels?

- Does the dealer let you demo components in the store?

- Will the dealer negotiate on price, or at least extend the warranty or offer extra support?

- Will this dealer meet and beat other dealers' prices?

- If local, will this dealer install and configure your upgrade?

- Is courteous, timely telephone support available (toll-free and extra hours, if it's a mail-order firm)?

- Does the vendor honor your right to a 30-day, money-back return?

- Does the warranty include parts and labor? Is there a no-questions-asked return/repair policy?

- If you wish to return your purchase, does the dealer levy a "restocking" fee?

- Does the vendor attempt to add a surcharge if you pay by credit card?

Notes:_____

_____

_____

_____

_____

_____

_____

Got a Mechanic? Some Basic, Step-by-Step Installation Tips

Ready for some fun? Here's the chapter that has you tapping on metal and wielding screwdrivers, pressing down parts and testing everything out.

Have a great time playing mechanic. Remember to take your time, be patient, be awake, and be in a well-lighted room. And (while you're being a Do-Bee) *do* read this entire chapter before you touch anything.

Tools to Have Ready

There are tools you *think* you need (witness the numerous kitchen cabinets that serve as appliance graveyards), and then there are the tools you can't live without. The following tools fall into the second category. These tools will see you through almost any upgrade.

- Phillips screwdrivers, small and standard sizes.

- Regular screwdriver, also called flathead, in a standard size.

- Pliers, standard type, standard size.

- Leadless mechanical pencil, or substitute a bent paper clip (for setting DIP switches).

- Notepad and pencil.

Never use a tool that's magnetic near your PC; magnetic fields can zap data for good! Check by seeing if your tool will pick up a screw; if it does, eschew that tool!

General Practices Before Any Upgrade

Clear off a desk, clean your room—do whatever makes you feel prepared for a project. Then perform these upgrade preliminaries. One more thing: Before performing any upgrade, *make sure you can always go back.* These safeguards will help you keep your peace of mind:

- Print out a list of all the directories/subdirectories on your hard disk.

- Keep your PC's setup information handy on a floppy disk. Copy all CONFIG.SYS and AUTOEXEC.BAT files to the disk as well.

- If you're adding a drive, know what type of drives you have. Each drive type is designated by a number that appears on the drive's external case and in its manual. This will be in your PC's setup program, as well.

The following are general steps to follow whenever you are working on your PC. You'll learn some specifics later in this chapter.

1. Exit any programs you're running.

2. Back up any data (you already did that the night before, right?).

3. Turn off your computer.

4. Turn off all peripherals connected to it.

5. Unplug your computer—at both ends, if you're really feeling nervous.

6. Unplug any peripherals—from the computer and from the power supply.

7. Clear off a large workspace.

8. Place all tools, a pad of paper, and a pencil near the work area.

9. Place your computer, its manuals, and any other extras that came with it, near the work area.

10. Remove the computer's casing, generally by unscrewing the outside screws with a Phillips screwdriver and sliding off the case, pulling it toward you. (The Dell and Amkly upgradable computers come apart with nice, easy thumbscrews.)

11. Without touching anything, study the inside of the computer. Make a mental picture of what's there. Consult Figure 16.1 for a generic look at a PC's innards and try to identify the major components inside *your* PC.

12. Perform the upgrade, as discussed in the appropriate section later in this chapter.

13. Before closing the PC's case, check the work area and count all the tools, making sure no tools or screws get left inside the system box.

14. Test the PC to ensure that the upgrade "took."

That's the basic procedure; you'll learn some specifics in the remainder of this chapter. Here are a few pointers that apply in all situations:

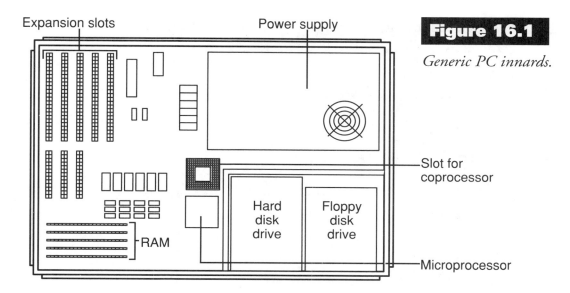

Figure 16.1

Generic PC innards.

Expansion slots

Power supply

Slot for coprocessor

Hard disk drive

Floppy disk drive

RAM

Microprocessor

NOTE

It's important to "ground" yourself frequently during the upgrading process to prevent static electricity from harming your components. To do this, tap the computer's power supply; this will discharge any static electricity.

- Ground yourself before handling cards or chips.
- Handle cards and chips only by their edges.

- When installing a new device, read the accompanying manual, no matter how impossible to decipher it appears.

- Be firm yet kind when pushing cards, chips, or other components into a slot. If it doesn't fit, don't force it!

Adding Memory

There's really nothing to adding memory, and it's probably the most popular upgrade among PC users.

1. Read your motherboard manual to see the configurations of memory chips it'll accept.

2. Buy memory chips in the appropriate size, speed, and configuration for your system. Memory comes in several different shapes, depending on the model of PC; some of these are shown in Figure 16.2.

3. Open your computer's case, paying attention to the general guidelines given earlier in this chapter.

4. Locate the memory bank on the motherboard, or on the memory card.

Figure 16.2

Memory comes in various shapes and sizes.

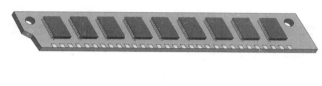

5. If there are old chips in the sockets you need to use, pop out the old chips carefully, lifting them straight out of their slots with your fingers. For example, if your computer uses SIMMs (small circuit boards), it would look like Figure 16.3.

Figure 16.3

Many PCs use memory that comes on small circuit boards called SIMMs.

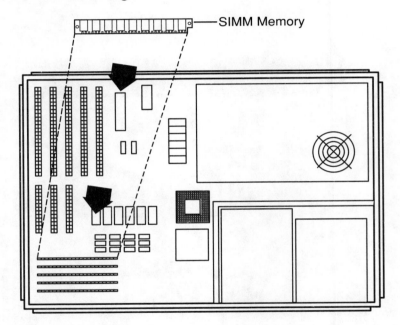

SIMM Memory

6. Hold the new memory over the appropriate socket.

7. Guide the memory into the socket, snap it into place, and make sure it's firmly seated.

8. If your motherboard manual indicates that it's necessary, change the settings of the DIP switches (locate them first, using your motherboard manual's diagram) to account for the new memory.

9. Before you replace the PC's case, turn it on and see if the upgrade "took"; watch for the memory check to appear on-screen. Then turn off the PC, hook everything back up, and run the CMOS program (next step).

10. Run your PC's setup program so your CMOS will take official note of your new RAM. (PCs differ greatly in how they invoke RAM.)

Jär-gen:

A DIP switch is a tiny on/off switch on a circuit card that controls a specific system setting. For example, some motherboards use DIP switch settings to tell the system how much RAM it should expect to be present.

How to Install an Expansion Card

Many upgrades require you to install an *expansion card*. These instructions will get you through just about any card.

1. Follow the preliminary steps and guidelines earlier in the chapter.

2. Without touching anything, look at your PC's expansion bus. How many 8-bit slots do you see? How many 16-bit slots? Do you see any 32-bit slots? You can tell the expansion slots apart by the length. The longer the slot, the higher the bit width. The 32-bit slots run the full length of the computer case. Be sure not to use up one of your larger slots on a small card. Make a sketch on your notepad of the slots that remain, and the size of each. This will come in handy for future upgrades.

3. Now, ground yourself. Do this by smartly tapping the unpainted side of the PC's metal framework or the power supply. Now that you're grounded, don't move your feet. And even though you're grounded, don't touch any parts on the motherboard, upgrade component, disk drives, power supply, and so on, unnecessarily.

4. With feet still, unwrap the expansion card from its protective packaging. Holding the card by its edges, examine it for any gross defects. Then put the card down gently on the work area.

5. Find the most suitable slot inside your PC. That is, find a slot that has the right size slot for the metal edge of the card to fit into. Choosing a slot that's too big wastes the slot's capabilities; if you choose a slot that's too small, the card won't work.

6. Look at the back "wall" of the PC. There you'll see a row of metal brackets, covering the "hole" at the back end of each unused expansion slot. Find the metal bracket that aligns with the slot you've chosen.

7. Carefully, so you don't drop the screw onto the motherboard (very tricky to find again and pick up), remove the screw holding the metal bracket in place.

8. Put down your screwdriver, and place the screw and bracket to the side of your work area, where they won't be lost.

9. Ground yourself again. Pick up the expansion card, hold it over the selected slot with the bracketed end facing the back "wall" of the PC, metal feet facing down (see Figure 16.4).

10. Position the card's metal "feet" into the selected slot. Gently rock the card back and forth, pushing gently until the card eases itself into the slot.

11. Screw the old bracket's screw into the expansion card's bracket. Save the old bracket in case you ever remove the card and want to cover the hole again.

12. *Carefully* power up your PC, and test to see if the new card is working right. If you're satisfied the upgrade "took," close everything up and hook up all the cables again.

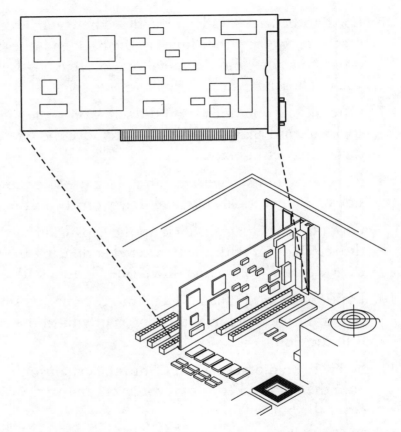

Figure 16.4

Placing an expansion card into a motherboard expansion slot.

13. Run any setup software that came with the expansion card. (You might want to review the section on software drivers, later in this chapter.)

Adding Microprocessor Upgrade Cards to Upgradables

A new breed of PCs is designed for the inevitability of upgrading, with ease of installation being the foremost design factor. Some offer snap-in microprocessor replacements, while a few models opt for the removal and replacement of a microprocessor expansion card.

Adding and removing such cards is almost identical to the process for typical expansion cards. The microprocessor card slot may or may not be on the expansion bus, depending on the manufacturer. Amkly PCs devote a special 32-bit slot on the expansion bus for their processor card. The Dell model I tested opted for a microprocessor slot off to the side. Both models featured special fans dedicated solely to cooling the main chip.

If you buy one of these PCs, chances are good you'll receive great documentation. Here are some steps based on my own findings:

1. Follow the preliminary steps given earlier in this chapter.

2. There may be a grounding wire attached to the processor card and to another component (on a Dell PC I tested, the grounding wire attached to the hard drive). Unscrew the wire from that other component, leaving it attached to the old microprocessor card. (The new card should come with its own grounding wire.)

3. Replace the old card with the new, and attach the new grounding wire to the hard drive or other component.

4. Be sure to push down very firmly. Gently rock the card at each end until both ends sit firmly in the slot.

5. Close the case, and power up your PC. The system should sense the new processor automatically. Make sure by watching the system monitor during boot-up, and noting which processor it says it has.

Dealing with Device Drivers

Many of the add-ons you can buy for your computer come with software disks that contain something called a *device driver* (in addition to other files and programs). A file on your PC's root directory called CONFIG.SYS tells your PC what hardware you want it to load up and get working. The mysterious filename stands for *configure system*, and does just about that. Adding a device driver is no more difficult than telling CONFIG.SYS where to find a file that controls that device.

We'll use a mouse in the example that follows, so if you have a different device (a CD-ROM drive or a scanner, for example), just substitute that in your mind when you read "mouse."

Some mouse software comes with an installation program that will create the directory for you; refer to your mouse documentation before going any further, because the steps here might not apply to your situation.

1. Make a subdirectory for the mouse software. A good place might be a MOUSE subdirectory under the SYSTEM directory: **C:\SYSTEM\MOUSE**, for example.

2. Copy the mouse's software into the mouse subdirectory.

3. Start a text editor program (your word processor will do, or DOS 5's EDIT program), and load the CONFIG.SYS file from your root directory.

DOS 5 comes with EDIT, a no-frills word processor of a type known as a text editor. Text editors are easy to come by on BBS systems or through friends. Often costing little or nothing, these programs make it easy to alter your system files. Programmers use them all the time.

4. Add a new line in your CONFIG.SYS file that reads:
device=c:\system\mouse\mouse.sys. (If your directory name or device name is different, use the appropriate names.)

Occasionally, a device's driver file will have a .COM extension instead of .SYS. If this is the case, you would add the line to your AUTOEXEC.BAT file rather than CONFIG.SYS. For example, for a .COM mouse driver, you might add:

C:\SYSTEM\MOUSE\MOUSE.COM

to your AUTOEXEC.BAT file.

5. Save the altered CONFIG.SYS file and exit the program. If you're using a word processor, make sure you save it as an *ASCII* or *plain text* file. Generally, you'll need to use the word processor's "Save As" command to save a file as plain text. Consult your user manual or on-line Help for more about ASCII text files.

6. Reboot your computer to load the device driver, and then test the device to make sure it works.

DOS 5 lets you "load" device drivers into high memory and conserve RAM for other uses. A typical command under this version of DOS would read: **devicehigh=c:\system\mouse\mouse.sys**. Consult your DOS manual for more ways to have fun with DOS 5.

How to Access Your PC's Setup Program

Many of the upgrade instructions in this book mention something about your PC's *setup program*. A setup program provides a way for you to tell a special type of PC hardware memory—the *CMOS memory*—what hardware changes you've made. You access it, change the settings, and then reboot your PC.

Although this all sounds unfamiliar (and perhaps a little scary), changing your setup basically means following a menu-driven program. In fact, the only difficult part about it is that each PC's manufacturer has found a different way for you to access the setup program. Otherwise, I could spell it out for you here. So find your PC's manual and look up your setup program. You might try accessing it just for practice. (Mine comes on-screen if I press **Ctrl+Alt+Esc** simultaneously after booting up. How about yours?)

Installing a SCSI Host Adapter

Remember the SCSI host adapter from Chapter 8? As with the other installations in this chapter, being *very* methodical helps here. Good luck!

May I See Some ID?

First, you'll need to assign each SCSI device a unique ID number. Simply push special buttons on an external device's rear, or flick switches on an internal device. Remember to tell your device driver software which number you've given the device. The host adapter will be (usually) device number 0. Although your adapter is quite willing to let any device take any number, some hardware manufacturers rigidly require that a device be granted a predetermined ID. Whatever you do, look up everything in advance and write down the numbers you assign to devices. And don't assign two devices the same ID number, or your SCSI chain will fail.

The Terminator

A SCSI device connects to the adapter, another device connects to the first, and so on. You'll need to decide what device will bring up the rear (if you're linking more than one), and single out this device by flipping its switches, jacks, or plugs in a ritual ominously known as *termination*. This prevents SCSI signals from bouncing off the end device and back into the cable. (Check your devices to make sure you don't need to disable pre-set termination, as well.) Just to complicate matters, if you install an internal SCSI device (a floppy drive, for example), this end of the chain will have to be "terminated" too, since the host adapter (which comes "terminated") is no longer considered to be at the end of the chain.

Connect the Devices

Link the devices firmly. Then power up the devices and reboot your PC. You'll want to install any drivers and other software for each device. After that, try out your new SCSI peripheral(s) with some software. What fun!

If at First You Don't Succeed . . .

If you've connected a single device, everything should work great. In the case of problems connecting multiple devices, first make sure you didn't assign two devices the same ID number. If that checks out, check for loose cable connections, or rearrange the cables altogether. You may have to select a different device as the end (terminated) unit. If all else fails, take each device and test it out alone with the host adapter and driver software. You may need to make a call to the host adapter vendor, to get assurance that their adapter brand is truly compatible with the device's brand.

Creating a RAM Drive with DOS

Now that we've ventured into devices that actually exist, let's try creating one that doesn't (but still works fine): a *RAM drive* or *virtual drive*. As you discovered in Chapter 3, the speediest "disk" is actually spare RAM that you dedicate to data or program storage. This RAM drive can benefit you if you're the type who saves files often, and you have plenty of free extended memory. Create a 512K disk by adding this line to your CONFIG.SYS file:

DEVICE=C:\DOS\RAMDRIVE.SYS 512K /e

RAMDRIVE.SYS is actually a mini-program called a *driver*, one of many included with plain old MS-DOS. This RAM device driver will set aside RAM with its own drive letter for storing files (if your highest drive letter is C:, the RAM drive will be D:).

To put the drive in expanded memory (if you're using spare RAM from an expansion card), replace **/e** with **/a**. Note that you must precede the line in CONFIG.SYS that installs your RAM drive with the line that installs your expanded-memory manager.

You can set up as many RAM disks during a particular working session as you want—just add a new line in your CONFIG.SYS file for each drive you want to create. The most effective way to use a RAM disk is to set up a TEMP environment variable, and point it to a subdirectory on the RAM disk; this can speed up programs like Windows that use temporary files. For details on this and many other ways to use a RAM disk, check out the RAM drive sections of your DOS manual.

Removing and Installing Disk Drives

Whether you're installing a floppy or hard disk drive, you'll follow the basic steps below. You'll want to retain some of your old data from the old drive, so be sure to back it up before you begin the upgrade. If you have a spare device bay, you may find it easier to install a new drive without removing the old one.

1. Follow the preliminary steps from earlier in the chapter. Remember to ground yourself.

2. If you are removing a hard drive, identify the one you're going to remove.

3. Remove the old drive's screws, which are found along the mounting rails. Put the screws to the side of the work area. See Figure 16.5.

4. Ease the old drive forward.

Figure 16.5

Hard drive fitted with mounting adaptor rails.

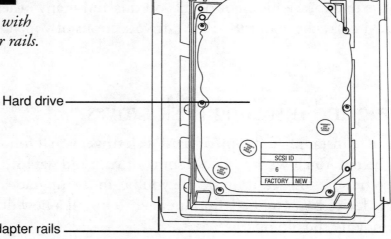

Hard drive——————————

Mounting adapter rails ——————

Jär-gen:

A strain-relief loop is a small loop of cable attached to the main cable. You can pull on it without fear of damaging the main cable.

5. Disconnect all cables. When you disconnect a cable, tug on its connector or on its strain-relief loop, *not on the cable itself.* Keep all connectors evenly aligned to avoid bending any connector pins.

6. Continue easing the drive out of the bay, and remove it. Set the old drive aside in the work area.

7. Remove the mounting rails from the old drive.

You can't open the drive's case, so don't even think about it.

8. Attach the mounting rails to the new drive.

9. Ease the new drive into place.

10. Make sure both connectors are correctly oriented and aligned. Then attach the cables.

11. Tighten all screws with a screwdriver.

12. Replace the computer's casing and reconnect all the cables.

13. Turn on the PC, and run its CMOS setup program to tell the PC about the new drive's type.

These same directions work for floppy drives too.

Making the New Hard Disk Ready for Software

Just physically installing your new hard drive is only half the upgrade process. In order to be able to work with software, including your disk operating system (probably MS-DOS), you need to perform the following:

- A low-level format.
- A disk partitioning.
- A high-level format.

Performing a Low-level Format

A disk must be *low-level formatted* to define tracks and sectors on it, grooves for your data, so to speak. Most disks you buy (particularly IDE-types) come with the low-level format already done. If you're not sure your drive has been low-level formatted, DOS comes with a utility called FDISK that can help you check. Consult your DOS manual for directions on how to use FDISK.

If you ran FDISK and it doesn't recognize the new hard drive, you need to perform a low-level format. The new disk comes with a floppy disk that contains the low-level formatting utility, a small program called HDSETUP or something very similar. Run this program according to the on-screen (or manual's) instructions, and you will perform your low-level format.

A few cards expect you to conduct the low-level format using DEBUG, a powerful program that comes with DOS. Proceed carefully, in this case, for you will be altering the hardware instructions on the hard drive controller's ROM chip. It's best to phone the place where you bought your hard disk, and either get them to low-level format it for you, or at least walk you through DEBUG on the phone.

Use FDISK to Partition Your Drive

Next you need to *partition* your hard drive. Think of partitioning as laying down one or more filing cabinets on your drive. DOS or another operating system will only feel at home on the new drive when they know what filing cabinet area they'll "live" in.

Insert a floppy disk that contains a backup of your MS-DOS files and utilities, and type the DOS command FDISK at the DOS prompt. (If you're adding a second drive, you won't need to run it from a floppy, but can run DOS from your hard disk prompt, as usual.)

You'll see a menu of choices; answer the questions according to how you want your disk set up. At this time, you can choose to partition the hard disk into one, two, or more *logical drives* ("C:" and "D:" for example), just by telling FDISK to do so. (But even if you want just one primary DOS partition on drive C:, you'll still need to run FDISK.)

Jär-gen:

A logical drive is different from the virtual, or RAM, drive you read about earlier in this chapter. The physical hard disk drive you buy is a certain size, say 100MB. After running FDISK from a floppy, you'll choose one or more drive areas where you can store data. Each separate drive area you set up on your real hard drive is called a logical drive. For instance, you could take your real hard drive's 100MB and divide it into a logical drive (or primary DOS partition, C:) of 50MB, and a logical drive (or secondary DOS partition D:) of 50MB.

A High-level Format

The hardware part's over, but you can't get crankin' on your new disk until your PC gives it an official Howdy! That's done through a process known as a *high-level format*. You will use software to perform this format: your computer's setup utility (usually a part of your PC's BIOS/CMOS, so it doesn't go away with your old hard disk), and MS-DOS's FORMAT and FDISK commands.

You're about to perform the scariest DOS command: FORMAT C:\. (And FORMAT D:\, if you've used FDISK to create a logical disk D:.)

You're familiar with FORMAT from readying floppy disks for use. Well, you also know that formatting a disk erases all the data on it. Erasing a floppy's not the end of the world (especially if you follow a sensible backup procedure). But erasing all the data on your hard disk? Shiver. Good thing there's no data on the new hard drive yet.

Run Your PC's Setup Utility

When you try to access the new drive, a DOS prompt will say **Cannot Access Drive C**, or something similar. Press the appropriate function key (or insert the proper floppy) to start your PC's setup utility. (All models differ; you're on your own here, so consult your PC's manual.)

Your setup screen will pop up, listing your PC's hardware specifications. (Some PC's can "autosense" whatever new hardware you stick inside, so the new info's already there, as on my Dell 450DE PC.) Make sure the specs for your new hard drive match those on the screen. If they don't match, consult your hard drive's manual, then type in the drive's new number, and whatever other information setup asks you for.

NOTE

The drive type—the one expressed as a number—is very important. If you specify the wrong drive type, you could have big trouble, either right away (your new drive won't work) or later (a year later your hard disk may choke for no apparent reason). The drive type is listed on a label on the new drive; double-check it before you enter the number in the setup program.

HISTORY

Most people are content with just having one "logical" hard drive, typically **C:**. However, many experienced users find that dividing their hard disk into two or more logical partitions helps to keep their files organized, and makes them look "cool" in front of their

continues

245

continued

friends. You could, for example, keep your system files and utilities on your **C:** disk and store Windows, programs, and games on **D:**.

But partitioning a disk isn't done just for aesthetics; earlier versions of DOS couldn't handle a hard disk formatted to more than 32MB. Bigger drives had to be partitioned into C, D, and even E to fool DOS. The current DOS version (5.0) can handle any partition size, but old habits linger . . .

A Final Note

Find a remote corner of your rec room or garage to use for storing boxes. If anything should go wrong and you need to ship a component back to the dealer or manufacturer, use its original case (and, if possible, the custom-fit padding) to pack it.

Notes: _____

_____

_____

_____

Glossary

While upgrading your PC, you'll probably come across some unfamiliar terms. Here's a guide to some of the jargon you'll encounter. For a more complete listing, look at the glossary in *The Most PC for Your Money*, the companion volume to this book.

386 nickname for 80386 microprocessor chip; a 386-based PC.

386DX a full-fledged 80386 chip; a PC powered by one.

386SX a 386 chip with external bus disabled, so it's more affordable; a PC driven by one.

486 nickname for 80486 microprocessor chip; a 486-based PC.

486DX a full-fledged 80486 chip; a PC powered by one.

486DX2/50 or 486DX2/66 computers using a recently introduced chip that doubles a PC's processing speed for internal chip tasks.

80386 the 80386 microprocessor; a PC based on this chip.

80486 the 80486 microprocessor; a PC based on this chip.

A

application another name for software that performs a task, such as a word processor or a spreadsheet.

B

baud used interchangeably with bps (not quite accurately) to measure a modem's transmission speed. Measures the number of transitions in the modem signal per second.

bit short for **bi**nary digi**t**; the smallest unit of data a PC processes.

bits per second (bps) measures number of bits of data moving to and from the CPU and other components; sometimes used in place of baud as a measurement of modem speed.

bus circuitry on a PC's motherboard by which data travels to and from the microprocessor.

byte measure of data quantity: eight bits make a byte; more commonly seen in thousands (kilobytes), millions (megabytes), or even billions (gigabytes).

C

CD-ROM short for Compact Disc-Read Only Memory, one type of PC storage.

central processing unit (CPU) primary chip, or microprocessor, inside a PC.

characters per second (cps) measures a dot-matrix printer's speed.

checksum verification routine common in serial communications; modems use a checksum to ensure transmitted data's integrity.

chip a silicone wafer that, when plugged into a circuit board, performs a useful function. RAM and microprocessors both come in chip form.

CMOS short for Complementary Metal Oxide Semiconductor, one or more chips used to keep track of the AT and better class of PC's hardware; a type of hardware memory you can alter with your PC's setup program.

COM short for communications, or serial, port; typically seen as COM1, COM2, etc.

communications software program you use to get your modem to communicate with other computers.

configuration a PC's particular hardware setup; sometimes refers also to software setup.

controller mechanism on a hard drive (or to which a hard drive is attached via expansion card or adaptor) that tells the hard drive what to do.

conventional memory the first 640K of memory in a PC.

D

data bus see *bus*.

device a monitor, keyboard, mouse, or any peripheral that can connect to a PC.

device driver a small program that enables the PC to work with a specific device plugged into it. Normally loaded at startup.

DIP short for dual in-line package, a RAM chip more commonly seen on older computers.

DIP switches toggle switches found on the motherboard and on expansion cards.

dots per inch (dpi) measure of resolution on monitors and printer output quality; higher is better.

download to bring data or program files into a PC, commonly through a modem, but can take place via other serial or parallel connection.

driver see *device driver*.

DX2 recent chip model that doubles PC processing for internal microprocessor functions.

Dynamic RAM (DRAM) the type of memory chip sold most commonly.

E

EISA   abbreviation for enhanced ISA, an enhanced model of system-bus architecture.

error correction   two modems enabled with this feature can double-check transmitted data between them.

expanded memory   RAM added through an expansion card (on 286 PCs and lower), or through software (on 386 PCs and above).

expansion bus   expansion slots on a motherboard.

expansion card   an add-on card for a new device like more memory, a mouse, or a modem; fits into an expansion bus slot.

extended memory   usable memory over 640K.

F

flash ROM   also seen as flash BIOS, allows the ROM BIOS to be updated electronically, to reflect hardware upgrades and other changes to a PC's configuration.

font cartridge   plug-in printer cartridge that adds new fonts to a printer.

forums   discussion areas focusing on specific topics, found on electronic bulletin board systems or commercial on-line services.

fragmented   hard-disk malaise where, over time, files are written to non-contiguous (spotty) locations, increasing seek time needed to access them.

G

game card   expansion card containing a special port for a joystick to plug into.

gigabyte   roughly a billion bytes.

graphics accelerator   video card equipped with chips to offload certain graphics processing tasks from the CPU.

graphics card   an expansion card that runs a monitor.

H, I, J, K

hardware   any physical equipment used in a PC configuration, from the PC itself to peripherals like a printer or a music synthesizer.

HST   the first major high-speed modem standard.

IBM PC-compatible   works with computers or chips of the IBM PC family.

IDE   a type of hard disk controller common in mid-size, low-cost drives.

inkjet printer   a non-impact printer that works by shooting ink blobs through dots.

interface card a serial or parallel board, also multifunction boards; usually already bundled inside a PC.

interlaced a monitor whose electron beams scan alternating lines; causes flicker that results in eye fatigue.

ISA the original system bus architecture of the AT-model PC; still a viable standard.

kilobyte (K or KB) approximately one thousand bytes.

L

laptop small, portable PC that weighs less than 12 pounds, generally powered by batteries while on the road and an AC adapter when not.

line noise phone line static; commonly found, but irritating in modem transmissions.

local bus enhanced expansion bus circuitry that provides direct data exchange between the CPU and expansion cards, speeding operation of that device; also video controllers that are wired right onto motherboard (less common).

luggable quasi-laptop, really too heavy to carry very far.

M

math coprocessor an add-on chip that takes some of the load off the microprocessor by performing arithmetic functions, including some graphics processing.

megabyte (M or MB) roughly 1 million bytes of data.

megahertz (MHz) 1 million hertz (or clock cycles) per second; measures speed of a CPU (higher numbers signal faster, more expensive, and more powerful CPUs).

memory usually seen referring to RAM, volatile memory; ROM, a permanent set of PC housekeeping instructions, is another type of memory.

memory card expansion card that lets you add RAM chips to it; best used after your PC's RAM slots are filled to capacity.

microprocessor the official name for the CPU, or main computer chip in the PC.

MNP4 a leading error correction standard for modems.

MNP5 a common data compression standard.

modem short for modulator/demodulator; scrambles a PC's data to enable transmission over ordinary phone lines, where a modem at the other end unscrambles the data for the receiving PC.

motherboard a large, green, printed circuit board "carpeting" the system box; provides framework for the CPU, expansion bus, memory chips, and all other parts of a PC.

Multimedia PC (MPC) standard for PCs which adhere to certain hardware requirements that enable them to work with multimedia software.

N, O, P

non-interlaced a monitor technology where the inner monitor surface is scanned all at once by electron beams instead of in alternating sections (as with older, interlaced models); minimizes flicker and eyestrain.

notebook current standard for power-and-price vs. size-and-weight for portable PCs.

on-line service any commercial service accessible via modem; CompuServe, Prodigy, GEnie, and America Online are a few examples.

organizers tiny, often non-DOS-compatible "computers."

OS/2 PC operating system offering an alternative to MS-DOS; though in development for many years, it has been slow to catch on.

pages per minute (ppm) measure of a laser printer's output speed; 6 ppm is average.

palmtops small portable PCs; offer tiny keyboards and displays; most are DOS-compatible.

parallel port extension of the PC's expansion bus; enables parallel devices to be connected to the PC; often called a *printer port*.

peripherals general term for any devices outside the actual PC system box.

ports gateways to your PC's innards so devices can connect to it; also called I/O ports; main types are parallel, serial, and SCSI.

power supply metal box inside the system box that supplies power to the PC; includes a fan for cooling purposes.

processor see *microprocessor*.

R

random access memory (RAM) volatile memory used as a temporary data storage tank by the micro-processor; data in RAM disappears into thin air when the computer's shut off. Lots of RAM is needed to run today's hoggish software.

read-only memory   see *ROM*.

refresh rate   monitor's top-to-bottom electron scan rate; also known as vertical scan rate; faster rates ensure less flicker.

RISC   short for Reduced Instruction Set Computer, a fairly new chip that processes data faster than the older CISC variety common on personal computers; found in fast laser printers.

ROM   short for read-only memory; a set of memory chips housing permanent instructions that tell a computer how to coordinate its various components and get to work.

S

scan rate   two types, vertical and horizontal scan rate, determine the monitor's overall quality; higher rates make for a better picture, less flicker, and less eyestrain.

serial port   connects to the motherboard by means of a serial interface card; provides a place to connect serial printers, mice, and modems, among other serial devices, to your PC.

setup program   a menu-driven program on your PC that's accessed at bootup; you can change the PC's specifications for your hard drive there, or tell your PC you've added more RAM, for example.

SIMM   RAM chip "card," a strip of three or nine DIP RAM chips; plugs into RAM expansion slots on the PC's motherboard. The dominant RAM chip/socket found on all the fashionable motherboards this season.

SIP   short for single in-line RAM chip "card" with pins, instead of the expansion card connectors found on the more common SIMM RAM module.

small computer system interface (SCSI)   high-end interface add-on to a PC's expansion bus; accommodates several SCSI devices at once (high-capacity hard drives or CD-ROM players, for example); faster under certain conditions than the parallel and serial interfaces bundled more commonly in a PC.

static RAM   a type of memory chip.

sub-notebook   this recent crop of portable PCs is smaller and lighter than notebook models, with possible compromises in keyboard size and display quality.

super VGA   a graphics mode that is quickly becoming the high-end standard; refers both to video card and monitor.

system box   the hard plastic case enclosing a PC's motherboard, power supply, disk drives, and other components.

T, U, V

termination   setting a SCSI device to be the end of a chain of similar devices.

tower   a vertical system box, usually large, with plenty of expansion slots and drive bays and an oversized power supply to cool all the goodies you can pack inside.

trackball   a pointing device housing a mounted ball and adjacent buttons; the cursor is manipulated by rolling the ball and pressing the buttons.

upgrade   to boost the power and versatility of a component (or an entire PC) by adding memory chips, a math coprocessor, a bigger hard disk, or other improvements.

upload   to send information from your PC to another PC through a serial device like a modem; see *download*.

V.32   an older, slower standard for modems, 9600 bps.

V.32bis   the new high-speed modem standard, 14400 bps.

V.42   an extension of the MNP4 error correction standard for modems.

V.42bis   the latest data-compression standard for high-speed modems.

V.fast   the "ultimate" modem standard, 28800 bps.

VESA   video-card manufacturer consortium that sets standards for high-end video modes, local bus, software drivers, and other PC video/graphics concerns.

Index

Symbols

386 chip, 247
386DX chip, 247
386MAX software, 54-58
386SX chip, 247
486 chip, 247
486DX chip, 247
486DX2/50 computers, 247
486DX2/66 computers, 247
80386 chip, 247
80486 chip, 247

A

Above Board memory board, 53
accelerator boards, 131
accessing setup programs, 235
accessories, assessment checklist, 23-24
Acer's ChipUp system, upgrading, 40
adapters, SCSI host, *see* SCSI
Advanced Gravis joysticks, 100
American Computer Exchange, 209
Amkly Systems upgradable PCs, 40, 222
applications, 247
Atari's Portfolio palmtop computers, 191

audio
    sound cards, 17-18
    ports, 179-180
AudioPort, 184

B

backing up
    hard disks, 36
    with Bernoulli drives, 77
    with floppy drives, 71-74
    with floptical drives, 76
    with magneto-optical drives, 77
    with tape drives, 19-20, 75-76
BACKUP utility, 36
batteries, portable computers, 199
    draining, 189
baud, 247
Bernoulli drives, 77
bits, 150, 247
bits per second (bps), 150, 169, 247
boot drives, 74
Boston Computer Exchange, 209
buffers, 65
    printer, 131
bulletin board systems (BBSs) run by
    mail-order vendors, 206-207

burst mode, 116
buses, 247
    expansion, 249
    local, 115-117, 250
Businessland, 205
buying
    CD-ROM drives, 181
    floppy drives, 72-74
    modems, 152-154
    notebooks and docking stations, 195
    PCs instead of upgrading, 27-29
    portable
        computers, process for, 187-188
        printers, 134-136
    SCSI host adapters, 102-103
    sound cards, 177
    through mail-order vendors, 206-209
    through stores, 204-205
    TV cards, 178
    used components, 209
    with credit cards, 213-214
bytes, 247

C

cache controllers, 65
caches, disk, 32-33
CAD (computer-aided design), 84
cards
    expansion, *see* expansion cards
    fax, *see* fax cards
    hard, 66-67
    interface, 250
    multifunction, 97
    port, 97-99
    RAM/ROM, 199
    video, 110-115
CD-ROM (Compact Disc-Read Only
   Memory), 16-17, 247
    drives, 178-181
characters per second (cps), 130, 248
checksums, 151, 248
chips, 248
    386DX, 247
    386SX, 247
    486DX, 247
    80386, 247
    80486, 247
    comparing types, 50-53
    DIP, 51-53, 248
    DX2, 248
    Dynamic RAM (DRAM), 248
    math coprocessors, 84-86, 250
    RISC (Reduced Instruction Set
      Computer), 252
    ROM, upgrading, 91-93
    SIMMs, 51-53, 252
    SIP, 52-53, 252
    upgrading, 82
ChipUp system, upgrading, 40
CHKDSK software, 35
CMOS (Complementary Metal Oxide
   Semiconductor), 248
co-processed video cards, 115

color
   portables, 198
   printers, 137-138
   video-card support, 111-112
.COM file extension, 234
COM ports, 248
commands
   BACKUP, 36
   CHKDSK, 35
   DEBUG, 242-243
   FDISK, 242, 243
   FORMAT, 244
   RESTORE, 36
Compatibility printers, 130
component-specific vendors, 209
compressing data
   sending over modems, 154
   software, 34
CompuAdd multimedia kit, 181-182
Computer Exchange Northwest, 209
computer-aided design (CAD), 84
ComputerLand, 205
CONFIG.SYS file, 232
configurations, 248
controllers, 64-65, 248
conventional memory, 248
CPUs (central processing units), 247
   checklist for adding, 94
   chips, upgrading, 82-84
   math coprocessors, 84-86
   motherboards, upgrading, 86-91
   ROM BIOS, upgrading, 91-93
credit cards, buying with, 213-214

D

data
   compression, sending over modems, 154
   transfer rate, 63
dealers
   buying with credit cards, 213-214
   checklist for asking, 215-216
   installation help, 210
   mail-order companies, 206-209
   reputation, 211
   service and repairs, 211-212
   shipping, 213
   stores, 204-205
   technical support, 212-213
   used components, 209
   warrenties, 212
DEBUG program, 242-243
Dell Computer systems, 208
   upgradable, 41-42, 222
Delrina's WinFax, 167-168
device drivers, 248
   installing, 232-235
devices, 248
Digital Equipment, 208
digital sound, 176
DIP (Dual In-line Package) chips,
   51-53, 248
DIP switches, 248
direct marketers, 208-209
discs, CD-ROM, 16-17
disk caches, 32-33
Disk Full message, 9

DiskTest software, 35
docking stations, 193-196
DOS
 RAM, 49
 version 5.0
  freeing memory with, 31
  memory management, 55
dot matrix color printers, 138
dot pitch, 118
dots per inch (dpi), 123, 130, 248
downloading, 148, 248
draft printing, 130
drive types, hard disks, 65-66, 245
drivers
 device, 248
  installing, 232-235
 RAMDRIVE.SYS, 37, 238-239
 software, 112
 SPEAK.EXE sound, 38
drives
 Bernoulli, 77
 CD-ROM, 16-17, 178-181
 floppy, *see* floppy drives
 floptical, 76
 hard, *see* hard drives
 logical, 243, 245-246
 magneto-optical, 77
 RAM (virtual), 32, 37-38
  creating, 238-239
 removing and installing, 239-246
 tape, 19-20, 75-76
Dual In-line Package (DIP) chips,
 51-53, 248

DX2 chip, 248
Dynamic RAM (DRAM), 248

E

earphone jacks, 179-180
Ecosys laser printer, 142
EISA (enhanced ISA), 249
EMS (Expanded Memory Specification), 55
enhanced mode, 56
Epson printers, 130
error correction, 151, 153, 249
ESDI (Enhanced Small Device
 Interface), 66
expanded memory, 55-56, 249
Expanded Memory Specification (EMS), 55
expansion buses, 249
expansion cards, 18-19, 53-54, 249
 game, 249
 graphics, 249
 hard, 66-67
 installing, 227-230
 local bus, 116-117
 memory, 53-54, 250
 microprocessor, installing, 231-232
 sound, 17-18, 175-177
 TV, 177-179
expansion stations, 193-195
extended memory, 56, 249
external
 CD-ROM drives, 179
 modems, 148

F

fax cards, 20-21, 162-163
    checklist, 171
    installing, 163
    reasons against, 166
    reasons for, 164-165
    software, 167-168
    terms, 168-170
faxes, 162-163
    sending from the road, 170
FDISK utility, 242-243
files
    backing up, 19-20
    CONFIG.SYS, 232
    extensions
        .COM, 234
        .PCX, 169
        .WAV, 38
filters, ozone, 142-143
fixed fonts, 130
flash ROM, 40, 93, 249
flatbed scanners, 123-124
flicker, 113
floating-point operations, 84
floppy drives
    adding, 71-72
    buying, 72-74
    portable computers, 199
    removing and installing, 239-246
floptical drives, 76
font cartridges, 131, 249

fonts, 130
    TrueType, 38-39
FORMAT command, 244
formatting hard drives
    capacity, 62-63
    high-level, 244
    low-level, 242-243
forums, 249
    vendor, 206-207
fragmented hard disks, 35, 249
frame buffers, 114
freeing memory, 31
full travel, keyboards, 197
full-height hard disks, 64

G

game
    cards, 249
    ports, 100
Gateway, 208
GeoWorks, 31
Gibson Research's SpinWrite defragmenting
    software, 35
gigabytes (GB), 48, 249
graphics
    accelerators, 249
    cards, 249
    scanners, 122-124
    still video units, 125
ground tracking numbers, 213
Group III-compatible fax cards, 170

H

half-height hard disks, 64
hand-held scanners, 122-123
hard cards, 66-67
hard drives, 61-62
    backing up, 36
    casing sizes, 64
    checklist, 68
    compressing, 34
    controllers, 64-65
    drive types, 65-66
    formatted capacity, 62-63
    fragmented, 35, 249
    high-level formatting, 244
    low-level formatting, 242-243
    MTBF (Mean Time Between
      Failures), 64
    optimizing, 35-36
    partitioning, 243
    portable computers, 199
    RAM (virtual) disks, 32, 37-38, 238-239
    removing and installing, 239-246
    running setup programs, 244-246
    size, increasing, 9-10
    speeds, 63
      increasing, 9-10
hardware, 249
    fax cards, 162-163
    math coprocessors, 84-86
    microprocessor chips, 82-84
    modems, 148
    monitors, 117-120

motherboards
    local bus, 115-117
    upgrading, 86-91
    port cards, 97-99
    ROM chips, upgrading, 91-93
    SCSI host adapters, 100-103
    switch boxes, 39
    video cards, 110-115
HDSETUP utility, 242
help with installation from dealers, 210
Hewlett-Packard
    HP LaserJet printers, 130
    HP95 series palmtop computers, 191
high memory, 49
high-level formatting, hard drives, 244
host adapters, SCSI, 100-103, 236-237
HPFS (High Performance File System), 36
HST (High Speed Transfer) protocol,
    157, 249

I

IBM
    mail-order, 208
    PC-compatibles, 249
    printers, 130
ID numbers, assigning to SCSI host
    adapters, 236
IDE (Intelligent Drive Electronics),
    65-66, 249
inkjet printers, 249
    color, 137

installing
  dealer help with, 210
  device drivers, 232-235
  disk drives, 239-246
  expansion cards, 227-230
  fax cards, 163
  math coprocessors, 86
  memory, 224-227
  microprocessor expansion cards, 231-232
  modems, 155
  ROM chips, 92-93
  SCSI host adapters, 236-237
  tools for, 219-220
Intel
  Above Board memory board, 53
  SnapIn, 28, 83
interface cards, 250
interlaced monitors, 250
interleave, 35
internal
  CD-ROM drives, 179
  modems, 148
interrupts
  assigning to ports, 104-105
  conflicts, 104
  requests (IRQs), 104
ISA, 250

J-K

joysticks, game ports, 100

keyboards, portable computers, 197
kilobytes (K or KB), 48, 250

Kingston Technologies
  chips, 83
  SX/Now! 286-to-386SX system
    upgrade, 28
Kraft joysticks, 100
Kyocera's Ecosys laser printer, 142

L

laptops, *see* portable computers
laser printers, 138-142
LaserTool's PrintCache print spooler, 32
letter-quality (LQ) printing, 130
line noise, 250
liquid crystal displays, portable computers,
  197-198
local buses, 250
  motherboards, 115-117
logical drives, 243
  multiple, 245-246
low-level formatting, hard drives, 242-243
luggables, 250

M

magneto-optical drives, 77
mail-order companies
  buying with credit cards, 213-214
  checklist for asking, 215-216
  component-specific vendors, 209
  direct PC sellers, 208-209
  gathering information about, 206-207
  general marketers, 207-208
  reputation, 211

service and repairs, 211-212
shipping, 213
technical support, 212-213
warranties, 212
Manifest diagnostics software, 105
math coprocessors, 84-86, 250
Mean Time Between Failures (MTBF), 64
Media Vision
   AudioPort, 184
   multimedia kit, 181-182
medium, 173
megabytes (M or MB), 48, 250
megahertz (MHz), 250
memory, 250
   adding, 224-227
   buffers, 65
   checklist for upgrading, 57-58
   conventional, 248
   disk caches, 32-33
   expanded, 55-56, 249
   expansion cards, 53-54, 250
   extended, 56, 249
   freeing, 31
   high, 49
   increasing, 8-9
   integrated helper utilities, 33-34
   management software, 32, 54-56
   print spoolers, 32
   RAM, *see* RAM
   ROM, *see* ROM
messages
   Disk Full, 9
   Out of Memory, 8

microprocessors, 250
   expansion cards, installing, 231-232
   upgrading, 82-84
   see also chips
milliseconds (ms), 63
MNP4 error correction standard, 250
MNP5 data compression standard, 250
modems, 148, 250
   bits, 150
   buying, 152-154
   comparison checklist, 158-159
   data compression, 154
   error correction, 153
   installing, 155
   line noise, checking for, 151
   modulating/demodulating, 150
   portable, 155
   speed, 152
   standards, 156-157
modes
   enhanced, 56
   printer, 130
modular, 6
monitors, 117-120
   checklist, 126
   interlaced, 250
   non-interlaced, 251
   software drivers, 121-122
   video cards, 110-115
motherboards, 251
   local bus, 115-117
   upgrading, 86-91
mouse, trackballs, 197

MTBF (Mean Time Between Failures), 64
multifrequency monitors, 119
multifunction cards, 97
multimedia, 173-174
    CD-ROM drives, 178-181
    checklist, 185
    elements, 174-175
    sound cards, 175-177
    TV cards, 177-179
    upgrade kits, 181-183
Multimedia PC (MPC) standard, 180, 251
multiscan monitors, 119
multitasking, 132

N

nanoseconds (ns), 52
near-letter quality (NLQ) printing, 130
non-interlaced (NI) monitors, 118, 251
Norton Utilities
    diagnostics software, 104
    DiskTest, 35
    Speed Disk defragmenting software, 35
notebook computers, 193, 251

O

on-line services, 251
    faxing services, 170
    vendor forums, 206-207
Optical Character Recognition (OCR), 169
optimizing hard disks, 35-36
organizers, 190, 251

OS/2 operating system, 251
    disk fragmentation, 36
    RAM, 50
Out of Memory message, 8
ozone filters, 142-143

P

pages per minute (ppm), 130, 251
palmtop computers, 191-192, 251
parallel ports, 251
partitioning hard drives, 243
PC Tools Compress defragmenting
    software, 35
PC-Kwik
    Power Disk defragmenting software, 35
    Power Pak integrated memory helper, 33
    SuperPC-Kwik disk cache, 33
PCs (personal computers)
    adding ports, 97-99
    accessing setup programs, 235
    anticipating future upgrades, 39
    assessment checklist, 12-13
    buying instead of upgrading, 27-29
    upgradable, 40-42
        installing microprocessor expansion
        cards, 231-232
    upgrading to multimedia standards,
        175-183
PCs Compleat, 207
.PCX file extension, 169
peripherals, 251
    assessment checklist, 23-24

pixels, 110
portable
   computers
      batteries, 199
      buying process, 187-188
      checklist, 201
      color, 198
      determining needs, 188-189
      displays, 197-198
      docking stations, 193-195
      hard and floppy drives, 199
      keyboards, 197
      laptops, 250
      luggables, 250
      notebooks, 193, 251
      palmtops, 191-192, 251
      RAM/ROM cards, 199
      sub-notebooks, 193, 252
      versus personal organizers, 190
   modems, 155
   printers, 134-136
   sound, 184
Portfolio palmtop computers, 191
ports, 251
   adding to PCs, 97-99
   audio, 179-180
   checklist for adding, 106-107
   game, 100
   interrupts, assigning, 104-105
   parallel, 251
   SCSI, 100-102
   serial, 252

PostScript
   emulation, 130
   printing standard, 130
Power Disk defragmenting software, 35
Power Pak integrated memory helper, 33
power supply, 251
print spoolers, 32, 132
PrintCache print spooler, 32
printers
   buffers, 131
   checklist, 144
   color, 137-138
   dot matrix, 138
   inkjet, 137, 249
   laser, 138-142
   ozone filters, 142-143
   portable, 134-136
   RAM boards, 132
   solid ink, 137-138
   terms, 130
   thermal, 138
   TrueType fonts, 38-39
   upgrading, 131-132
programs, *see* software
protocols, *see* standards

Q

Qualitas' 386MAX software, 54-58
Quarterdeck
   Manifest diagnostics software, 105
   QEMM software, 54-58

R

RAM (Random Access Memory), 8-9,
  47-48, 251
  amounts needed, 48-50
  cards, portable computers, 199
  chips, comparing types, 50-53
  counting, 50
  DRAM (Dynamic RAM), 248
  drives, 32, 37-38
    creating, 238-239
  print spoolers, 132
  printer boards, 132
  saving by running multiple programs
    in Windows, 31
  static, 252
RAMDRIVE.SYS driver, 37, 238-239
refresh rate, 113, 118, 252
repairs, dealer service, 211-212
reputation, dealers, 211
resolution, 110
RESTORE utility, 36
returns, shipping, 246
RISC (Reduced Instruction Set Computer)
  chip, 252
ROM (read-only memory), 252
  BIOS (Basic Input-Output System)
    memory self-test, 50
    upgrading, 91-93
  cards, portable computers, 199
  flash, 40, 249

S

saving RAM, 31
scalable fonts, 130
scan rate, 252
scanners, 122-124, 169
SCSI (Small Computer System Interface),
  66, 252
  host adapters, 100-102
    buying, 102-103
    connecting devices, 237
    ID numbers, assigning, 236
    terminators, 236-237
    troubleshooting installation, 237
self-test, ROM-BIOS, 50
serial ports, 252
  increasing with switch boxes, 39
service, dealers, 211-212
setup programs, 252
  accessing, 235
  running at hard-drive installation,
    244-246
Sharp's Wizard personal organizers, 190
shipping merchandise, 213-214
  returns, 246
SIMMs (Single In-line Memory Modules),
  51-53, 252
SIP (Single In-line Package) chips,
  52-53, 252
SnapIn
  386, 83
  upgrade products, 28

software
  BACKUP, 36
  CHKDSK, 35
  compression, 34
  DEBUG, 242-243
  Delrina's WinFax, 167-168
  drivers, 112
    for video cards and monitors, 121-122
  fax cards, 167-168
  FDISK, 242-243
  GeoWorks, 31
  Gibson Research's SpinWrite
    defragmenting, 35
  HDSETUP, 242
  integrated memory helpers, 33-34
  LaserTool's PrintCache print spooler, 32
  Norton Utilities
    diagnostics, 104
    DiskTest, 35
    Speed Disk defragmenting, 35
  PC Tools Compress defragmenting, 35
  PC-Kwik
    Power Disk defragmenting, 35
    Power Pak integrated memory helper,
     33
    SuperPC-Kwik disk cache, 33
  Qualitas' 386MAX, 54-58
  Quarterdeck
    Manifest diagnostics, 105
    QEMM, 54-58
  RAMDRIVE.SYS, 37, 238-239
  RESTORE, 36
  setup, 235, 244-246, 252
  Stac Electronics' Stacker compression, 34
  system, upgrading, 30-31
solid ink color printers, 137-138
sound
  cards, 17-18, 175-177
  drivers, 38
  portable, 184
SPEAK.EXE sound driver, 38
speed
  expansion cards for Windows, 18-19
  hard disks, 63
  modems, 152
SpinWrite defragmenting software, 35
spoolers, print, 32
Stac Electronics' Stacker compression
  software, 34
standards
  High Speed Transfer (HST), 157, 249
  ISA, 250
  MNP4 error correction, 250
  MNP5 data compression, 250
  modem, 156-157
  Multimedia PC (MPC), 180, 251
  V.32, 157, 253
  V.32bis, 157, 253
  V.42, 253
  V.42bis, 253
  V.fast, 152, 157, 253
  VL-Bus, 116-117
static RAM, 252
still video units, 125

storage
    Bernoulli drives, 77
    checklist, 78
    floppy drives, 71-74
    floptical drives, 76
    magneto-optical drives, 77
    tape drives, 75-76
stores
    buying with credit cards, 213-214
    checklist for asking, 215-216
    reliability, 204
    service and repairs, 211-212
    shipping, 213
    technical support, 212-213
    types, 204-205
    warranties, 212
sub-notebook computers, 193, 252
super VGA, 252
SuperPC-Kwik disk cache, 33
switch boxes, 39
SX/Now! 286-to-386SX system upgrade, 28
synthesized sound, 176
system
    box, 252
    software, upgrading, 30-31

T

tape drives, backing up with, 19-20, 75-76
technical support, 212-213
terabytes, 48
termination, SCSI host adapters,
    236-237, 253

text editors, 233
thermal color printers, 138
thin-film transistor (TFT) active-matrix
    displays, 198
tools for upgrade installations, 219-220
Toshiba, 208
towers, 253
trackballs, 197, 253
troubleshooting SCSI host adapter
    installation, 237
TrueType fonts, 38-39
TV cards, 177-178

U

U.S. Robotics' High Speed Transfer (HST)
    protocol, 157
upgrading, 4-5, 253
    anticipating future upgrades, 39
    for multimedia, 175-179
    low-cost tricks
        backing up hard disks, 36
        compressing hard disks, 34
        integrated memory helpers, 33-34
        memory, 31-33
        optimizing hard disks, 35-36
        RAM disks, 37-38
        SPEAK.EXE sound driver, 38
        switch boxes, 39
        system software, 30-31
        TrueType fonts, 38-39
    memory, 224-227
    microprocessor chips, 82-84

monitors, 117-120
motherboards, 86-91
objections to, 4-7
PCs (personal computers)
    installing microprocessor expansion
      cards, 231-232
    to multimedia standards, 175-183
    upgradable systems, 40-42
ports, adding, 97-99
preliminaries, 220-224
printers, 131-132
reasons for, 7-11
ROM BIOS, 91-93
system software, 30-31
tools for, 219-220
video cards, 110-115
when not to, 27-29
    checklist, 44
uploading, 148, 253
USA Flex, 207
used components, 209
utilities, *see* software

V

V.32 modem standard, 157, 253
V.32bis modem standard, 157, 253
V.42 standard, 253
V.42bis standard, 253
V.fast modem standard, 152, 157, 253
vendors, *see* dealers
vertical scan rate, 113, 118

VESA, 253
    compatibility, 113
VGA cards, types, 114-115
video
    accelerator cards, 114
    cards, 110-115
      checklist, 126-127
      software drivers, 121-122
    local bus motherboards, 115-117
    still units, 125
virtual drives, 37-38
    creating, 238-239
VL-Bus standard, 116-117

W-Z

warranties, 212
.WAV extension, 38
Western Computer Exchange, 209
Windows
    expansion cards, 18-19
    RAM, 49
      saving by running multiple
        programs, 31
    TrueType fonts, 38-39
    version 3.1 SPEAK.EXE sound
      driver, 38
    workstations, 42-43
WinFax fax software, 167-168
Wizard personal organizers, 190

About the Author

Tina Rathbone has covered education, technology, and consumer issues for six years as a writer and editor. Currently, she runs her High-Performance Communications business from her home computer, where (when she's not struggling to keep her cat off the keyboard) Rathbone is testing the latest in home computing and small-business applications for a variety of consumer publications. She also writes about scientific and technical computing, as well as herb gardening, food, and travel.

Rathbone is the former editor of *Supercomputing Review*, a monthly magazine covering the high-performance computer industry. She has also been the editor of *ComputerEdge Magazine*, as well as CPE books, where she enjoyed chronicling the delicate interplay between humans and machines.

Learn computers the easy way with PC Novice!

Learning to use computers is like anything new — getting started is the hard part. Now there's a computer magazine designed specifically to help you get started. It's called PC Novice — the only magazine that presents *Personal Computers In Plain English*. Every issue of PC Novice is packed with articles that explain the basic information you need to learn how to use your PC.

Need advice on how to computerize your business?

PC Today helps small businesses solve problems with computers. With pertinent article topics and an easy-to-read editorial style, PC Today keeps you entertained as well as informed. It's the best way you can find out about hardware and software that will give your growing business a competitive edge.

BUSINESS REPLY MAIL

FIRST CLASS   PERMIT NO. 10   LINCOLN, NE

POSTAGE WILL BE PAID BY ADDRESSEE:

PCNOVICE

P.O. BOX 85380
LINCOLN, NE 68501-9807

NO
POSTAGE
NECESSARY
IF MAILED IN THE
UNITED STATES

UPGRADE CHECKLIST

Fill out this checklist to summarize what you have learned in this book about your system's upgrading needs. Not all blanks will apply to you, since you will not need to upgrade every component in your computer. Then tear out the checklist to take with you when shopping.

PART I: Existing System

Motherboard Brand and Type: _____

Installed RAM: _____

Expandable to: _____

Type of RAM chips needed: _____

Microprocessor brand and type: _____

Coprocessor slot open? _____

Existing video card brand and type: _____

Existing video memory: _____

Room for more RAM on video card? _____

Existing monitor brand and type: _____

Existing printer brand and type: _____

Room for more RAM in printer? _____

Other existing components: _____

PART TWO: Desired Components

Software needed (type, purpose, brand, other specifications): _____

RAM type needed (type, speed, capacity): _____

Memory card needed (type, capacity): _____

Memory management software needed: _____

Hard drive needed (type, capacity, speed, other factors): _____

Other storage media needed (floppy drives, CD-ROM, tape backup, removable hard drive, etc.): _____

Microprocessor replacement needed (type, brand, any compatibility issues): _____

Coprocessor needed (type, brand): _____

New motherboard needed (brand, type, expansion slots needed, case size it must fit into): _____

_____

_____

New ROM BIOS chips needed (type, manufacturer):

_____

_____

Ports needed (how many of each: parallel, serial, game, SCSI): _____

_____

Type of port expansion card desired (manufacturer, number of ports, card size): _____

_____

Video card needed (brand, model, colors/resolution required, compatibility issues): _____

_____

Monitor needed (brand, model, colors/resolution, dot pitch, other issues): _____

_____

_____

Scanner needed: (brand, model, quality, scanning area size, ability to read text): _____

_____

Printer upgrade needed for existing printer (accelerator board, RAM, font cartridges, etc.): _____

_____

New printer needed (manufacturer, model, speed, quality, special features desired): _____

_____

Modem or fax/modem needed (speed, compatibility, error correction, fax capability, other special features): _____

_____

Multimedia equipment needed (CD-ROM, sound board, speakers, software): _____

_____

Is the above an integrated package or separate components? _____

Type of portable PC needed? (consider microprocessor, drives, display, connectivity, battery life, etc.):

_____

_____

Other: _____

_____

_____

_____